GERMANY

1944

—

The British Soldier's Pocketbook

With a foreword by
Charles Wheeler

and an introduction by
Edward Hampshire

the national archives

*The National Archives gratefully acknowledges
the generous help of Sue Seber
in the development
of this book*

First published in 2006 by

The National Archives
Kew, Richmond
Surrey, TW9 4DU, UK
www.nationalarchives.gov.uk

The National Archives (TNA) was formed when
the Public Record Office (PRO) and Historical Manuscripts
Commission (HMC) combined in April 2003

Foreword © Charles Wheeler 2006
Introduction © Edward Hampshire 2006

A catalogue card for this book is available from the British Library

ISBN   1 903365 91 0
978 1 903365 91 5

Cover design, page design and typesetting: Ken Wilson | point918
Printed in Germany by Bercker

CONTENTS

FOREWORD

It was when we crossed the Dutch frontier—at Venlo, some 40 miles northwest of Cologne—that we knew Hitler had lost his war. The German countryside was a sea of white flags; pillow-cases, featherbed covers, towels, anything white, hanging from the upstairs windows of every house. Germany's civil population was giving up on the *Führer*, opting to capitulate, using free choice for the first time since 1933.

We could see why when we reached Cologne. Shredded by the bombers, the city was one big road block. In the distance, as lonely as a lighthouse and apparently intact, was the cathedral. Every street leading into the town was clogged with chunks of broken buildings; and somewhere under the rubble heaps women, children and elderly men were living in burrows.

We'd been told to expect resistance after Germany's defeat. Snipers and booby traps. Bands of roving 'werewolves'. Yes, there were a few fanatics. Driving north towards Bremen, we caught up with the advanced reconnaissance unit of the Guards Armoured Division. One after another, their leading tanks had been knocked out by boys of 15 firing bazookas from nearby bushes. But this was the Wehrmacht's very last stand. By now Allied troops were counting their prisoners in hundreds of thousands.

How to cope with that unwieldy haul was the British army's biggest headache. On the last day of April 1945, serving with the Royal Navy's Forward Intelligence Unit, I was spending an evening at an improvised prisoner-of war cage when the BBC announced

Hitler's death. The 'camp' was open farmland enclosed by coils of barbed wire. It had rained for three days; there was a biting wind; and some 3000 prisoners were up to their ankles in mud, soaked to the skin. I suggested telling the Germans the news. 'They're probably too miserable to care', said the major in charge. 'But go ahead.' So, from the top of a truck, its headlights on to get them to listen, I called for quiet. '*Ruhe!*' And, still in German: 'Some news from London. Your *Führer* is dead. It was suicide.' For several seconds, dead silence. Just below me a single POW started clapping. Slowly it spread, a chorus of applause, all across that sodden field.

What none of us had expected from the Germans was their complete acceptance of defeat. This really was unconditional surrender. For the next 12 months I was based in Hamburg, where several British families, including mine, had lived and worked before the war. Until we left Germany in 1938 we'd had neighbours who were Nazis and neighbours who detested the system. Not surprisingly, the Nazis were now in denial. A typical reunion could go like this: 'As I am sure you will remember we were only nominal Party members. One had one's wife and children to consider. I would like to emigrate to Ipswich. Perhaps you can help? Please give me a cigarette.'

In spite of such encounters, I disliked and disobeyed orders from Whitehall to treat all Germans as suspects. Yes, millions of Germans were devoted to Hitler. But Nazi Germany was a savage police state, and it took more than ordinary courage to kick against the pricks. We soon found out that there had been more active wartime resistance to Hitler than the British establishment was willing to acknowledge, just possibly because to concede this would have clashed with the doctrine—implicit in the pocketbook reprinted here—that the Germans were innately war-loving, psychologically crippled and born to be bad.

Sixty years later it is hard to imagine what the troops can have made of these instructions for their behaviour. (In my case the distributors scored a miss.) I imagine most British soldiers would have skipped the bit about Bismarck, enjoyed the language lesson ('Spitting forbidden') and scanned the 'Security Notes' at the end in complete disbelief:

> Don't be too ready to listen to stories told by attractive women. They may be acting under orders. Germans must still be regarded as dangerous until the final Peace Settlement has been concluded *and after the occupation of Germany has ended.* [my italics]

The authors of the pocketbook, of course, were policy-makers —politicians, civil servants and senior military men. Their booklet mirrors the orders laid down in Whitehall and followed by the British occupation authority at least until 1948. The problem wasn't just that during interviews with British officials Germans were made to stand; that in towns every German was required to give way to British officers by stepping into the roadway; or that our soldiers risked detention if they gave a child a piece of chocolate. (Many of the more rigorous rules were ignored, and later relaxed.) What did persist for much too long, however, was the refusal of the victors to accept known anti-Nazi men and women as partners who could help them run the country.

Christabel Bielenberg, an Englishwoman married to a German, was a close family friend who had lived in Germany before and throughout the war. Her husband, Peter (who was imprisoned by the Gestapo after the abortive attempt to assassinate Hitler), and several of their friends were active members of the opposition. Returning to London at the end of the war, and with the help of David Astor, editor of the *Observer*, Mrs Bielenberg set up a meeting with senior civil servants and offered to put them in touch with proven anti-Nazis who had survived. Her idea was to build up a network of trustworthy Germans who would cooperate with British officials on the ground. The offer was never taken up. It was as though the men who tried to kill Hitler were felt to be particularly dangerous, she told me later. After all, they were plotters.

Such institutional prejudice against all Germans was enormously wasteful. Very few of Britain's 24,785 Control Commission officials running the British occupation zone spoke German or knew the country. The Americans adopted the opposite approach, seeking out Germans they could rely on and recruiting Jewish refugees. They were keen to get their own people home, of course. The result was striking. The number of Americans running the US zone of Germany at the end of 1946 was a modest 5008.

Charles Wheeler
May 2006

INTRODUCTION

A few minutes after 9 p.m. on the 23rd March 1945, four battalions of soldiers from the Gordon Highlanders, Black Watch and Argyle and Sutherland Highlanders crossed the Rhine in amphibious craft, landing close to the small German town of Rees. Nine and a half months after the Allied landings of D-Day, this Rhine crossing marked the first part of the Allied assault into the German heartland. It was also the first time that British soldiers had crossed the German Rhine in wartime since the 18th century. Resistance was initially relatively heavy, but within four days a bridgehead 35 miles wide and 20 miles deep had been created and over 30,000 British soldiers were over the Rhine and advancing into Germany.

Combined with American thrusts south of Wesel and from Remagen and Oppenheim, Canadian advances through the Northern Netherlands and the massive Soviet assault from the East over the Oder, the crossing of the Rhine marked the beginning of the closing stage of the six-year war with the Nazi Third Reich. Coordinated German resistance collapsed, and within three weeks US and British forces had reached the Elbe. Within a further three weeks, Berlin had fallen, Hitler had committed suicide and Allied forces had reached the Danish, Czech and Italian borders. Germany had been utterly defeated and hundreds of thousands of troops, one of whom was this writer's grandfather, were now occupying the defeated Reich.

To attempt to prepare British soldiers for their tasks as occupiers, each one was given a small paperbound guide to Germany and the

Germans, entitled simply *Germany*. This booklet is reprinted here, in its entirety. It was created by the Political Warfare Executive (PWE), a branch of the Foreign Office and the government's enemy propaganda unit. In 64 pages it provided, among other things, a short history of Germany, the reasons for the war and the occupation, and an explanation of 'what the Germans are like'. It also included a short phrasebook with phrases ranging from the inevitable 'Give me your papers' ('Geben Sie mir Ihre Papiere') to the wonderfully polite 'Can I park here?' ('Kann ich hier parken?').

The pocket guide was intended to condition, as far as possible, soldiers' thoughts and behaviour in the situation they would find themselves, where, in the guide's words, they would 'meet a strange people in a strange, enemy country'. It should be remembered that few ordinary British soldiers would have even travelled abroad before, and now they would be living not only with foreigners but former enemies to boot.

Germany must be viewed as a product of a specific historical moment, representing the beliefs, hopes and prejudices of the individual officials, propagandists and military officers who wrote it. At times unintentionally humorous and sweepingly generalist in its assertions, it deals with a range of social and political matters specific to the planned occupation; but the guide also serves to open a window onto the wider cultural assumptions and political priorities of wartime Britain and its public servants.

Dividing the German pie. At the Yalta conference of February 1945, Churchill, Roosevelt and Stalin had decided to divide a defeated Germany into separate zones, each occupied by one of the victorious Allies. Britain was allocated the northwest of Germany, including the trading centres of Hamburg and Emden, the historic city of Hanover (home of the British monarch's 18th-century ancestors) and Bonn, a medium-sized Rhineland city that would become the capital of West Germany.

Unlike at the end of the First World War, the victorious powers would this time invade and fully occupy Germany. In the eyes of some, the lack of an occupation in 1918, and therefore the lack of a visible manifestation of military defeat, encouraged former German soldiers in the belief that they had been 'stabbed in the back' by weak politicians—a belief that the Nazis had exploited. The Allies did not want to make the same mistake twice, and just as crucially Stalin wanted nothing less than the complete occupation of Germany. The Allied advance across Germany therefore followed the planned sectors that each ally would occupy. The British and Canadians advanced northeast to the lower Elbe and on the Danish border, the Americans pushed south into Bavaria and east to the upper Elbe where their sector would be, and the Russians moved westwards to meet the British and US forces.

Montagu Butler writes a memo. The British government had been quietly planning how to run propaganda and the media in territory liberated from the Axis powers as early as December 1942. A small committee, with the suitably Orwellian name of the 'Political Disarmament Sub-Committee of the Law Committee', was created. It was made up of officials from the Ministry of Information, the Political Warfare Executive, the Foreign Office and the War Office. This committee began to discuss how the German machinery of information and propaganda—from schools to radio and newspapers—might be controlled after the war had ended. It was not until the late spring of 1943 that the committee began to supervise detailed planning being undertaken by the Political Warfare Executive.

The first suggestion that British troops should be given some guidance came from Nevile Montagu Butler, a First World War veteran and head of the Foreign Office's North America desk. In a short note of 22nd May 1943, and while admitting that the production of such guidance was 'quite outside my competence', he was forthright that British soldiers should be given something to counter the views and arguments of the Germans with whom they would inevitably come into contact:

> Having sampled in 1914–1915 and to a less[er] extent in 1919–1920 the mesmerism of German propaganda that is diffused by the common people of Germany from the fact that they are allowed to see no news, and have no thoughts but what is officially given to them, I am somewhat obsessed by what may confront our troops when they come to occupy German territory, and am most anxious that steps should be taken in advance to counter the danger.

Taking a particular example, Montagu Butler believed that:

> … the Germans take a sort of sneaking pride in their robust treatment of the Jews; it is most desirable that our troops should take them up sharply on this, making it abundantly clear

that we have regarded the Jewish persecution as nauseating
and barbarous.

If 'robust' sounds far too mild a description of the Holocaust, it
should be remembered that the reality of the Nazis' 'Final Solution'
was not yet widely known or accepted in 1943 (and indeed the
final guide never would prepare soldiers for barbarities of that
level). Butler also urged that the guidance be as concise as possible so that it could be easily remembered.

Planning a 'Soldier's ABC'. Montagu Butler's note was passed
to Peter Ritchie Calder, head of Plans and Campaigns at the
PWE, whose staff had, at almost the same time, begun the
detailed planning of the control of the German media following
occupation. Calder was an interesting man for the job: a committed socialist and pacifist, he had come to prominence for
his coverage of the London Blitz for the BBC in 1940 and was
recruited to the PWE a year later.

One of several recommendations of a short paper written by
the Executive a few days after Butler's note was that a 'Soldier's
ABC for Germany' be written for distribution to all British
occupying troops. By August John Hawgood, one of Calder's
colleagues and an academic specializing in German–American
relations, had produced a two-page draft introduction [National
Archives, FO 898/480, folios 272, 273]. This early attempt at the
first few pages of the proposed ABC mentioned all the core
elements that would form part of the final version. The draft
included possible section headings for the ABC, descriptions of

Germany and the Germans, an outline of German politics, a small phrasebook, and a series of answers to questions from Germans.

Most significantly at this early stage, there was the same awareness, apparent in later drafts and the final guide, of the need to tread a difficult line. That line was between preventing soldiers from sympathizing too readily with Germans and therefore accepting their arguments and justifications for the war and their brutal treatment of minorities (the case made by Butler)—and, equally important, preventing soldiers from treating the Germans with brutality or complete indifference. Hawgood began his draft by explaining that:

> There are many different types of Germans. Not all of them are Nazis, but they have all lived under a ruthless Nazi dictatorship for over ten years, and as a result the way they think and act may at times seem very strange to you—like persons who have been suffering from a mysterious disease of the mind or from the influence of drugs. A very large number of Germans welcome[d] the Nazis and supported or condoned everything they did. Most of the others shrugged their shoulders and decided that there was nothing they could do about it, even when all their rights and liberties were taken away from them and they saw innocent people persecuted and tortured by Hitler and his gang. Most Germans are therefore what we call 'accessories before' or 'accessories after the fact' of the Nazi crimes and terrorism.

This was strong and uncompromising language, and it made absolutely clear his view that most, if not all, Germans were in some way responsible for Nazi crimes and the war itself. However, his final paragraph summed up the other side of the equation:

But don't be tough with the Germans just for the sake of being tough. Don't behave in an arbitrary way, and be just with them at all times—even when you have to be severe. They will respect you for this. They have not seen much of democracy or of justice lately. At first they may not even recognise them when they see them. Help them to learn and you may be doing something very solid towards saving the world from yet another German war.

'The vices of militarism and aggressiveness'. Hawgood's concerns and forthright language are clearly mirrored in the foreword to the final version of *Germany*. Although none of Hawgood's original words survive, the tone definitely has. A draft of December 1943 was even more severe, informing British servicemen that they:

> … will be told many hard-luck stories and see many pitiful sights. Some of the stories will be true, but many will be hypocritical attempts to play on your feelings. For, taken as a whole, the German is brutal when he is winning, and is sorry for himself and whines for sympathy when he is beaten. [National Archives, FO 898/480, folio 199]

This description of the German 'national character', ludicrously crude from a modern viewpoint, was elaborated elsewhere in the final guide, which stated that the reasons for the war dated back even to the creation of the German state in the period up to 1871:

> Remember this: for the last hundred years—long before Hitler— German writers of great authority have been steadily teaching the necessity for war and glorifying it for its own sake. The Germans have much to unlearn.

The argument that the roots of German behaviour under the Nazis originated in the century before Hitler was expressed in forceful terms that came close to suggesting that a German state did not deserve to survive. After crediting Bismarck, the Prussian statesman, with uniting Germany, 'the vices of militarism and aggressiveness, often thought to be peculiar to the Prussians, soon infected the whole of Germany'.

These last words had also appeared in the December 1943 draft, and none of the comments by the various officials and military officers suggested a toning down of these conclusions; in some instances a stronger line was advocated. As late as November 1944 a note from the Control Commission, the body that would run the British zone of postwar Germany, was suggesting that:

> ... the pamphlet as a whole appears to overstress the responsibility of the Nazis and to under-emphasise the degree of militarism and militarist propaganda (e.g. in the schools under Weimar) which was being conducted long before the Nazis came into power. [National Archives, FO 898/480, folio 201]

The Control Commission even argued that a section should be inserted in the guide stating that even before the Versailles Treaty had been signed in 1919, the German General Staff, industrialists and many civil servants were already planning a 'war of revenge'. In contrast, Robert Walmsley of the PWE urged caution:

> ... it would perhaps be unwise for us to assert positively that the German General Staff was not thinking or writing about this subject since that is the normal function of any General Staff in any country. We should, however, avoid giving the impression

that German policy at that time was already aimed at another war since it is extremely unlikely that the readers of our booklet would be ready to swallow this. [National Archives, FO 898/480, folio 204]

The Control Commission's suggestion was not in the end included.

A view from across the pond. For its own armed forces, the United States had already prepared a similar guide, and a comparison between the British and US versions reveals interesting divergences in experience and attitude. In terms of the issue of 'war guilt', the overall effect of the American guide on the reader is to emphasize the impact of the Nazi regime, the blame attaching to it for the war, and the contrasting liberal democracy that preceded it. In other words, the US guide avoids the British stress on the legacy of German militarism.

The reasons for this difference are not hard to account for. By 1944, Britain had suffered nine years of brutal war with Germany out of the previous thirty years, enabling a perception of an inevitably expansionist and militaristic nation to become rooted. In contrast, for the United States, with its significant population of German immigrants and their descendants, blaming the war specifically on the Nazis rather than Germans in general had been an important part of building support for the European war. And of course, the United States had not been engaged in war for so many years, had not suffered the numbers of casualties or the existence of a 'home front' subjected to bombing and potential invasion, and had not been economically devastated by the war.

'A hornet's nest all to himself'. The imprint of bureaucratic infighting within the Political Warfare Executive itself can also be detected in the approach of the British guide to the 'militarism' of German society. The roots of this can be traced to the appointment of a brilliant but argumentative and insubordinate Oxford academic to head up the Germany Section of the PWE in 1941: Richard Crossman. Later a cabinet minister under Harold Wilson in the 1960s, he was appointed in 1941 under the patronage of Hugh Dalton, Minister for Economic Warfare. He rapidly began to collect enemies among his colleagues despite their acknowledgement of his intellectual and propaganda skills.

Described by one former colleague (cited in Ellic Howe's book, p. 5, see below) as being less a stirrer of hornets' nests than 'a hornet's nest all to himself', Crossman inevitably made an enemy of F.A. Voigt, the PWE's leading Germany adviser before Crossman's arrival. Voigt wrote a stinging memo to the Foreign Office prior to his resignation from the PWE, roundly criticizing Crossman. Voigt argued that by emphasizing the culpability of the Nazis and by trying to drive a wedge between Nazis and other Germans, Crossman was actually pushing Germans towards Hitler while also ignoring the (at best, passive) acceptance of Nazism by the ordinary German (see Howard's book, pp. 88–9).

A safe pair of hands. Eventually Crossman was seconded by the PWE to Algeria in early 1943, to be replaced by Duncan Wilson, who, after the whirlwind of Crossman was undoubtedly seen as a very capable 'safe pair of hands'. From the same Winchester

School and Oxford University background as Crossman, Wilson had initially been refused entry to the Foreign Office in the 1930s after failing the medical, but the necessities of war solved that. After the war he would become one of the Foreign Office's leading authorities on communism and the Eastern bloc, his career culminating as ambassador to the Soviet Union in 1968–71.

Wilson's Germany Section of the PWE would oversee the writing and production of *Germany*, and it is not surprising, given the extreme reactions that Crossman had engendered across the PWE and Foreign Office, that there was a return to Voigt's earlier emphasis on German/Prussian militarism. Wilson's general approach can be best summed up in a comment he made to an officer in the Army's public relations office, the Bureau of Current Affairs: 'I feel strongly that re-education [of the British] about Germany is more important than re-education of Germans' [Duncan Wilson, National Archives, FO 2/10/44, folio 77]. For Wilson, though, this task of understanding the Germans better, and learning to counter the apologies for Nazism that soldiers and occupation officials would meet, was also vital to a successful rehabilitation of the German people and state. He would spend much of the last years of the war spreading this message through lectures and papers given to the Control Commission for the British sector, the body that he would join himself in May 1945.

There was also a strongly pragmatic element to Wilson's approach: education of the Germans through the example of fair, restrained and informed British occupiers would be cheaper, easier and probably less counter-productive than attempts at a direct mass re-education effort of the 80-million-strong German nation.

Compiling the first draft. Hawgood's draft foreword of August 1943 had provided the initial tone for the Germany guide; but a framework, consistent with other guides being concurrently written on France and Italy, needed formulation. A month later, the committee at the PWE responsible for the various country guides set out the framework within which *Germany* would be written. In addition to a physical description of Germany and a brief overview of German history, the guide should also include sections on what the people are like, what the war has done to them, what the Germans think of the British, and practical facts about life in Germany—from the womenfolk to sport and food [folios 147 and 153]. The writers under Wilson began to work within these parameters and the guide itself was fully drafted in less than three months. It is worth looking at how the writers addressed each of the areas in turn.

Fair-haired lovers of uniforms. The guide's characterization of the average German is perhaps not surprising given its emphasis on a militaristic culture. Thus there are the generalizations that appear absurd and simplistic to modern eyes, such as 'if you have to give orders to German civilians, give them in a firm, military manner. The German civilian is used to it and expects it' or 'the Germans adore military show. In Nazi Germany everyone has a uniform'. However, there is also a hint that in these sentiments the guide was preparing the soldiers to be confident in giving the

directions and orders that they, as representatives of the occupying power, would be expected to give to the German military
and civil authorities. In fact, such language had actually strength-
ened during drafting on the recommendation of Brigadier Erich
Sachs, the Director of Political Warfare Intelligence, who asked:

> … is the excessive attention which Germans automatically pay
> to uniforms brought out clearly enough—or the need for our
> soldiers to regard themselves and act as superior to all German
> uniforms, e.g. police etc?

Going beyond the matter of German respect for uniforms, the
guide also suggested that the German nation as a whole was not
too far from being psychologically unhinged. The first draft stated
that the German:

> … mixture of sentimentality and callousness does not show a
> well-balanced mind. The Germans are not good at controlling
> their feelings. They have a streak of hysteria. You will find that
> the German may often fly into a passion if some little thing goes
> wrong, wave his arms and become quite incoherent.
> [National Archives, FO 898/480, folio 135v]

In the published *Germany*, most of the above remained.

The crude physical stereotyping of average Germans, suggesting
that 'they look like us, except that there are fewer of the wiry type
and more big, fleshy, fair-haired men and women', also says much
about the writers' assumptions about 'us', i.e. a physically and
racially homogeneous readership. In fact, Brigadier Sachs's personal assistant made a point about the 'Anglo-centric' nature of
the early drafts. He noted that:

> … some reference should be made to them [the Canadians and other British Commonwealth forces] (however trivial) when referring to 'English climate', 'British troops', 'British Women'. It seems an un-important point to people in this country but it is of vast importance to them. The Germans are only too ready to look for weaknesses and faults in our relations with the Dominions … [National Archives, FO 898/480, folio 128]

Some concessions to this matter were made, but important phrases, given emphasis in the final text, still state that 'while you are serving in Germany you are representatives of Britain' rather than the British Commonwealth.

American 'gangsters'. An interesting alteration in the final version was a change, on the instructions of Brigadier Sachs, in the description of how Germans supposedly viewed the Americans [National Archives, FO 898/480, folio 127]. The first draft stated:

> The Germans think of the Americans much in the same ways as they think of us, but they do not know them so well and some of their ideas are rather odd. Americans, they think, are rich but uncultured, and many of them make their living as gangsters.
> [National Archives, FO 898/480, folio 137v]

In the final version the sentence was made a little more discreet so as not to offend the United States: 'Many of their ideas [about Americans] come from Hollywood films, which were once very popular in Germany.' The guide continues by noting that 'their first idea of the American troops as "amateur" soldiers has been completely disproved by battle experience'.

'What the Nazis have done to the Germans'. The section first entitled 'What the Nazis have done to the Germans' was reduced in size significantly during the development of the guide. The first draft of October 1943 contained brief but colourful descriptions of some of the senior Nazi leaders. Goebbels was a 'a depraved dwarf with a club foot, who, as German Propaganda Minister was responsible for making all Germans think alike' while the foreign minister Ribbentrop was dismissed as a 'champagne salesman' who 'advised Hitler that the British would swallow any affront because we were too decadent to fight' [National Archives, FO 898/480, folio 133v]. This draft section has a cross in pencil marked against it in the relevant file at the National Archives. Although no explanation of its removal has been found, its exclusion is not surprising.

These were pieces of very crude (though not wholly inaccurate) propaganda that did not sit well with the tone of much of the rest of the guide. Such words were good for lifting morale and ridiculing the enemy during wartime; but the soldiers reading the guide would most likely be occupying a defeated country, and descriptions of this type ran the risk of undermining the credibility of the rest of the guide.

Another significant excision was the cutting of a couple of paragraphs, also at the end of the section, entitled 'a word of advice'. Assuming that the Nazi system had collapsed following occupation, the reader was asked: 'to whom can you apply for information in case of need?' The rhetorical answer given was: 'the police'. The draft continues:

> The ordinary policeman (Schupo), though he was under Himmler's orders, did not change very much. He will probably be carrying on when you arrive. If it is not a matter for the police, apply to the Mayor (Burgermeister). [National Archives, FO 898/480, folio 196]

In a terse response, the Control Commission's rejoinder in November 1944 was: 'The ordinary (Schupo) did not change much! He did not need to, and many of them are now SS men' [National Archives, FO 898/480, folio 233]. The PWE protested that it had followed the available expert advice when the draft had been written, but to no avail. The section was deleted.

Fraternizing with the enemy. The language regarding fraternization with German women is perhaps some of the strongest in the guide and eventually (*see below*) reflected the policy adopted by the military leadership, the Supreme Headquarters Allied Expeditionary Force (SHAEF). The soldier-readers were informed that 'venereal diseases are prevalent', that one in four adults under 41 had the disease, and that 'numbers of German women will be willing, if they can get the chance, to make themselves cheap for what they can get out of you'. To modern eyes, the tone seems overwrought in its alarmism. Even at the time some people voiced concerns about such schoolmasterish attitudinizing. Robert Walmsley noted early in the drafting that the guide appeared to have a 'slightly patronising air at present', though he added that it 'may be unavoidable' [National Archives, FO 898/480, folio 143, Walmsley to Wilson].

The British guide at least had the advantage of consistency in its comprehensive bar on fraternization. In comparison, the US guide offered contradictory advice that might have done little but confuse soldiers. The opening pages of the American guide seemed to rule anything out:

> There must be no fraternisation. This is absolute! Unless otherwise permitted by higher authority you will not visit in German homes or associate with Germans on terms of friendly intimacy, either in public or in private. They must never be taken into your confidence.' [National Archives, FO 898/480, folio 31v, Pocket Guide to Germany, p. 2]

However, when it came to a section called 'marriage facts' the guide took a more ambiguous attitude:

> Now that you are on foreign soil, you should know that marriage to a foreign girl is a complicated procedure. Before you get too romantic remember that foreign girls do not automatically become citizens upon marriage to an American.

How a soldier would have the chance of 'getting romantic' when he was not allowed in theory to fraternize at all is difficult to imagine. The US guide continues:

> It takes three years of residence in the United States before she can even take the examinations. In any case, you cannot marry without the authorisation of your commanding officer. Even with this permission, you would have difficulty getting your wife back to the U.S. since there are no provisions for transporting dependents during wartime, nor are there likely to be for a long time to come. [National Archives, FO 898/480, folio 39, Pocket Guide to Germany, p. 18]

Perhaps surprisingly, the sexually transmitted diseases that so vexed the British compilers make no appearance in the US version. A tacit acceptance that short-term liaisons would be inevitable, natural urges being ungovernable by a rule book? The differing treatments of this subject again say more about the cultures and intentions of the British and American compilers than they do about Germany at the end of the war. Implicitly, the US guide seemed to be drawing a distinction between short-term sex (unofficially tolerated) and long-term marriage (positively discouraged), whereas in British eyes the former had the horrible potential to lead to the latter, so had to be nipped in the bud. For good measure, the British guide offers some melodramatic scenarios of miserable Anglo-German married life.

A soldier's *Baedeker*. Many sections of the British guide read more like a blunt travel guide for backpackers: advising on the excellence of German sausages and beer (the latter being the 'pleasantest in Europe'), the inferiority of some of their hot beverages ('the Germans don't know how to make tea') and the potency of their spirits ('the cheaper sorts are guaranteed to take the skin off one's throat'). In sport, the Germans are 'keen and capable performers', with football being the most popular game, although not played professionally. (How times have changed.) The British soldier, presumably in the event that he finds himself in a game of football with Germans, despite the strict bar on fraternization, is given the helpful advice that 'charging is regarded as rough play'.

A short description of the architectural highlights of Germany mentions the beauty of Naumburg, Hildesheim, Speyer, Bamberg and Worms cathedrals, although it is admitted that Cologne Cathedral has 'suffered in raids'. Throughout the rest of the guide the effects of Allied bombing are, however, bluntly set out: 'you will see areas that consist largely of heaps of rubble and roofless, windowless shells.' That German cities had suffered much greater devastation than their British counterparts is also made clear. One insertion late into the final drafting of the guide provided the example of Duisburg, which suffered from the dropping of more ordnance on it in one two-day raid than London suffered from September 1940 to July 1941.

In a 'question and answer' section of the early drafts, which was never included in the final guide, the deliberate targeting of civilian targets in the RAF's strategic bombing campaign is, however, steadfastly denied as a 'myth of Nazi propaganda'. Rather, 'it is an unfortunate fact that military and industrial targets are generally in thickly populated areas'. Moreover, in an attitude of 'they did it first', the guide states that: 'The German air attacks on Warsaw, Rotterdam and Belgrade were designed as a measure of pure terrorism and took place before our heavy bombing of Germany began' [National Archives, FO 898/480, folio 246].

In fact, it is not clear whether all the drafters of the guide were aware of the full reality of the bombing strategy; but those that did know did not feel that British soldiers should be made aware of it, even though they would be spending months or years walking through its effects in the bombed-out cities.

Last-minute objections. The drafting of *Germany* was completed by December 1943 and distributed to the relevant sections of government. The responses were positive from the Foreign Office, the office of SHAEF, Military Intelligence, and the Ministry of Economic Warfare. Ritchie Calder congratulated Wilson on the work he and his team had put in [National Archives, FO 898/480, folio 108]. One disappointment was that Winston Churchill's office had refused a suggestion that the prime minister write the final foreword for the guide. Churchill's private office gave an imperiously dismissive reply: 'The Ministerial view is that this is not really the kind of document to carry a message from him. He has demands made on him from all sides. We should reserve our request for a bigger occasion than this' [National Archives, FO 898/480, folio 107]. Given the invocation of 'the Ministerial view' by the author, it is unlikely the note even reached as far as Churchill.

From January 1944 until September of that year, the guide remained in limbo, awaiting the approach of British troops to the German border before printing of the planned 400,000 copies would start. However, as British troops embarked on the Arnhem campaign and Montgomery promised to be in Berlin by Christmas, the Military Section of the nascent Control Commission for the future occupied Germany got hold of early circulating copies. The Control Commission persuaded Victor Cavendish-Bentinck, Chief of the Joint Intelligence Committee, to halt printing plans until the guide fell in with SHAEF non-fraternization policy.

In fact, this was a cover for the Military Section's real concerns.

The main worry of General West of the Control Commission was about the tenor of the guide regarding the guilt of the Germans as opposed to the Nazis. Even though the replacement of Crossman by Wilson at the PWE had ensured a stronger stress on a long-standing German militaristic culture (as described above), this was not far enough for the Control Commission. General West interpreted the guide as the application of the dangerously soft 'naughty Nazi' theory. West noted that: 'The assumptions are, in fact, typical of a German left-wing refugee and whoever wrote the pamphlet seems at least in part to have adopted that point of view' [National Archives, FO 898/480 folio 232]. The PWE indeed had a reputation for being worryingly left-wing within Whitehall and the military ever since it had come under the wing of Hugh Dalton. Not only had it employed some German émigrés, its idiosyncratic recruitment policies had brought in such 'dangerous' figures as academics and BBC employees, and Richard Crossman had epito-mized this stereotype.

What threatened to descend into a tedious bureaucratic turf war was stopped short by the increasing urgency of starting the printing process and agreeing on a finalized draft. The Control Commission was able to enforce changes in some sections of the guide; but it is also clear that West did not get all the changes that he wanted. Having discovered the widespread praise across departments that the guide had garnered, the Control Commis-sion backtracked from much of its original position.

A changing world. *Germany* was finally printed in late 1944 and early 1945. The British soldiers who carried these small pamphlets, whether helping to conquer Germany or occupy it afterwards, were taking part in one of the great pivotal points in 20th-century history. As the ordinary soldiers' experiences on the ground came to replace the preconceptions and hypotheses of the guide, the whole context of their mission as an occupying force was beginning to change, from establishing authority over one defeated enemy to squaring up to a new, challenging one.

In late 1946 increasing British and American suspicion of Soviet intentions and aims resulted in the decision to form 'Bizonia', combining two of the three western zones of occupation in Germany. A year later the Marshall Plan provided US support for economic reconstruction in Europe, but the Soviets and the states they occupied pointedly refused to take part. The Soviet Union was antagonized by the creation of a new currency, the Deutschmark, for the western zones. And the thorny issue of the divided Berlin resulted in the Soviet blockade of that city and the successful Anglo-US response of the Berlin Airlift, which gave the besieged West Berliners their lifeline. So it was that the rubble of an occupied Germany, which the readers of this guide came upon as occupiers, formed the crucible of the 40-year-long struggle of the Cold War.

Sixty years on, in a separate struggle, British soldiers are again an occupying force in the land of a defeated regime. It will be interesting, in years to come, to see how far the guidance they were given matched the reality they encountered.

NOTES ON SOURCES AND FURTHER READING

A mixture of books and original documents was used to write this introduction. For the history of the Political Warfare Executive *The Black Game: British Subversive Operations against the Germans during the Second World War* by Ellic Howe (London: Michael Joseph, 1982) and *The Secret History of PWE: The Political Warfare Executive, 1939–1945* by David Garnett (London: St Ermin's, 2002) are the definitive accounts. Anthony Howard's biography of Richard Crossman (*Crossman: The Pursuit of Power*, London: Cape, 1990) also provides illuminating material on the PWE during Crossman's time there. Patricia Meehan's *A Strange Enemy People* (London: Peter Owen, 2001) illuminates the British occupation.

Most of the primary material came from files at the National Archives, and one in particular: FO 898/480 'Pocket Guide for Invasion Forces: Germany'. This file contains, in addition to much internal correspondence relating to the guide, copies of various drafts, including the first full draft of October 1943 (folios 129–41) and penultimate draft of mid-1944 (folios 184–99), as well as a copy of the US equivalent (folios 30–54). Other files provided valuable background detail: FO 898/478, 479 and 481–83 are similar files relating to the creation of guides for other occupied countries; FO 898/365 provides useful material on the Political Disarmament Sub-Committee of the Law Committee.

Edward Hampshire
Modern Records Specialist, The National Archives

GERMANY

This book has nothing to do with military operations.

It deals only with civilian life in Germany and with the way you should behave to the German civilian population.

This book is published in November, 1944, at a time when our Armies have barely entered Germany and Hitler and the Nazi regime have not yet been overthrown. Many important events may happen between now and the time when you first read this book. Do not be surprised therefore if here and there sentences, true at the time they were written, have become out of date.

GERMANY

CONTENTS

FOREWORD

FOR the second time in under thirty years, British troops are entering upon the soil of Germany. The Germany Army, the most carefully constructed military machine which the world has known, has suffered catastrophic defeats in the field. The civilian population of Germany has seen the war brought into its homes in a terrible form. You will see much suffering in Germany and much to awake your pity. You may also find that many Germans, on the surface at least, seem pleasant enough and that they will even try to welcome you as friends.

All this may make you think that they have learned their lesson and need no further teaching. But remember this: for the last hundred years—long before Hitler—German writers of great authority have been steadily teaching the necessity for war and glorifying it for its own sake. The Germans have much to unlearn.

They have also much to atone for. Never has murder been organised on so vast a scale as by the German Government and the German Army in this war. Death by shooting, hanging, burning, torture or starvation has been visited on hundreds of thousands of civilians in the countries of Eastern Europe occupied by the Germans, and on thousands in the occupied countries of Western Europe.

The record of these outrages is not just "atrocity propaganda." It is based in most cases on the evidence of eye-witnesses or on statements made by the criminals themselves.

Moreover, the writings and speeches of the German leaders show that such outrages formed part of a deliberate policy.

The German people as a whole cannot escape a large share of responsibility. The main instruments of German policy were certainly Hitler's Black Guards and Secret Police, but ordinary German officers, N.C.O.'s and men acted often enough with the same brutality. Individual German soldiers and civilians may have deplored it, but no one was found to protest publicly and in good time against it. From the time Hitler came to power no serious resistance movement showed itself in Germany until the attempted putsch of the German generals on the 20th July, 1944. But the cause of that revolt was not the barbarity of Hitler's methods, but merely their lack of success.

The history of these last years must not be repeated. The purpose of the British Commonwealth and its Allies, and of the forces which represent them, is not vengeance against the Germans. It is to make sure that they will never again have the chance to submerge Europe and the world in blood. Remember for as long as you are in Germany that you would not be there at all if German crimes had not made this war inevitable, and that it is only by the sacrifice of thousands upon thousands of your fellow countrymen and Allies, and at a cost of untold suffering at home and abroad through five long years, that British troops are at last on German soil. Think first of all this when you are tempted to sympathise with those who to-day are reaping the fruits of their policy, both in peace and war.

TO BEGIN WITH—

YOU are going into Germany.

You are going there as part of the Forces of the United Nations which have already dealt shattering blows on many fronts to the German war-machine, the most ruthless the world has ever known.

You will find yourselves, perhaps for some time, among the people of an enemy country; a country that has done its utmost to destroy us—by bombing, by U-boat attacks, by military action whenever its armies could get to grips with ours, and by propaganda.

But most of the people you will see when you get to Germany will not be airmen or soldiers or U-boat crews, but ordinary civilians—men, women and children. Many of them will have suffered from overwork, underfeeding and the effects of air raids, and you may be tempted to feel sorry for them.

You have heard how the German armies behaved in the countries they occupied, most of them neutral countries, attacked without excuse or warning. You have heard how they carried off men and women to forced labour, how they looted, imprisoned, tortured and killed. THERE WILL BE NO BRUTALITY ABOUT A BRITISH OCCUPATION, BUT NEITHER WILL THERE BE SOFTNESS OR SENTIMENTALITY.

You may see many pitiful sights. Hard luck stories may somehow reach you. Some of them may be true, at least in part, but most will be hypocritical attempts to win sympathy. For, taken as a whole, the German is brutal when he is winning, and is sorry for himself and whines for sympathy when he is beaten.

SO BE ON YOUR GUARD AGAINST "PROPAGANDA" IN THE FORM OF HARD-LUCK STORIES. Be fair and just, but don't be soft.

You must also remember that most Germans have heard only the German side of the war and of the events that led up to it. They were forbidden to listen to any news except that put out by their own Propaganda Ministry, and were savagely punished if they disobeyed. So most of them have a completely false impression of what has happened, and will put about—perhaps in good faith—stories that are quite untrue.

The impression you have gained of world events is much nearer the truth than the distorted conceptions spread by the German Propaganda Ministry. So don't let yourself be taken in by plausible statements.

Of course there are Germans who have been against the Nazis all along, though few of those who tried to do anything about it have survived to tell the tale. Even those Germans who have been more or less anti-Nazi will have their axe to grind. But there is no need for you to bother about German attempts to justify themselves. All that matters at present is that you are about to meet a STRANGE PEOPLE IN A STRANGE, ENEMY COUNTRY.

5

Your Supreme Commander has issued an order forbidding fraternisation with Germans, but there will probably be occasions when you will have to deal with them, and for that reason it is necessary to know something about what sort of people they are.

THE GERMAN LAND

GERMANY is a big country.

In area it is twice as big, and in population about one and a half times as big, as England, Scotland, Wales and Northern Ireland together.

As the map on pages 32 and 33 shows you, Germany is landlocked except for the tideless Baltic in the north and a short coastline on the North Sea. In the east and west its frontiers are not defined by great mountains and rivers, which is one reason perhaps why the Germans are always trying to push them further out.

Its greatest rivers, the Rhine, Elbe, Oder and Danube, are not purely German, since they flow through other countries before reaching the sea.

The climate in North-Western Germany is rather like that in Britain, but as you go south or east you will find it hotter in summer and colder in winter than it is at home. There is more rain in Western Germany than in the east, but everywhere you will get more fine, hot days in summer and more crisp, bright cold in winter.

Germany has a great variety of scenery. In the north is a great plain, bare except for occasional pine forests and studded with lakes; it is a continuation of the plains of Russia and Poland. In Central Germany the hilly uplands are thickly forested. The valley of the Rhine with its sudden hills, its vineyards and old castles, is well known to English tourists, and further south you come through the foothills to the German Alps.

Industry. Germany is highly industrial. The German "Black Country" is in the west on the Rhine and Ruhr, where what is left of the towns of Cologne, Dortmund, Düsseldorf, Duisburg, Essen, Bochum and many others familiar from our Air Ministry reports, form one great continuous industrial area. Other great centres of manufacture are in Thuringia and Saxony (Central Germany) and in the eastern province of Silesia.

The north-western port of Hamburg, which is about half as big again as Glasgow is probably the most "English" of German towns. It has always had close commercial ties with this country.

Seventy years ago, Berlin, the capital, was about the size of Manchester. Now, with a population of nearly four and a half millions, it is over one-third as big as Greater London. It is the seat of government of the German "Reich" and is practically surrounded by a broad belt of industrial plants.

The German transport system was one of the best in

Europe. Apart from its excellent railways, much use was made of the great natural waterways, like the Rhine, which were connected by a system of canals. One of Hitler's positive achievements was to build hundreds of miles of first-class motor-roads, though his object in doing so was largely military. These are called *Autobahnen* (car-ways).

THE GERMAN STORY

THE most interesting fact about German history is that GERMANY DID NOT EXIST AS A NATION UNTIL 1871. Before then it consisted of a number of states each with its own court, its own laws and customs barriers. Much the largest of these states was Prussia.

The credit (if one can use the word) for uniting these various kingdoms and grand duchies belongs to a Prussian statesman, BISMARCK.

BETWEEN 1864 AND 1871 HE ENGINEERED THREE AGGRESSIVE BUT SUCCESSFUL WARS against Denmark, Austria and France, and these victories so impressed the other German States that they entered a confederation under Prussian leadership. This confederation was called the German Reich, and the King of Prussia became German Kaiser (Emperor).

The vices of militarism and aggressiveness, often thought to be peculiar to the Prussians, soon infected the whole of Germany. The Germans acquired colonies, chiefly in Africa; they challenged British sea-power by building a powerful fleet. And in 1914 they thought they were strong enough to enforce an unchallenged supremacy in Europe. In alliance with Austria-Hungary, Turkey and Bulgaria they fought and lost the First World War.

After the defeat of 1918 Germany went through a sort of revolution. This revolution was largely lath and plaster, but was accepted by the Germans because they are used to political shams. Some of the politicians of the German Republic, who succeeded the Kaiser in 1918, meant well: they established a parliamentary system which gave to the ordinary German more individual freedom from then to 1933 than before or since. But behind the scenes the real power still remained in the hands of the generals, the great industrialists and landowners and the professional civil servants. They waited and watched for a chance to assert themselves.

The chance came with the rise of Adolf Hitler.

Rise of Hitler. This ex-corporal of the First Great War was not even a German, but an Austrian who had fought in a German regiment. At first he was considered rather a joke, but his party, the National Socialist German Workers' Party (Nazi for short), gained millions of supporters during the great slump of 1930–32. He promised the workers a form of socialism; he promised the industrialists more power and bigger profits; he promised both that he would wipe out the Versailles Treaty and create a single "Great German" State. The Nationalist Party (Junkers—that is, feudal landowners

—generals and industrialists) believed they could use the Nazis to restore their old privileges. So they persuaded the President, Field Marshal von Hindenburg, to make Hitler Chancellor of the Reich. This was in January, 1933.

To secure his election in March, Hitler engineered the Reichstag fire and by attributing it to the Communists made it the excuse for a reign of terror. But the elections in March did not give Hitler's party a clear majority, in spite of the flood of propaganda let loose in his favour from platform, press and radio; the Nationalists, however, supported him, and to make doubly sure he arrested various members of opposition parties who might have voted against him.

His next act was to pass a bill which ended parliamentary government and made him Dictator of Germany.

Then he began to "discipline" the country. Law was suspended. Jews, Communists, Socialists, Liberals—anyone who had publicly opposed him—were hunted down by Hitler's private Army, the Storm Troops, shot, beaten to death or systematically tortured in concentration camps. HITLER'S AIM WAS SO TO TERRORISE THE GERMAN PEOPLE THAT NO ONE WOULD DARE TO RESIST HIM BY DEED OR WORD.

In spite of these bestial cruelties some Germans were brave enough to carry on the struggle against Hitler, but their power was small and most were killed, beaten into acquiescence, or forced to leave the country.

Meanwhile the army was rapidly growing; in 1935 conscription was reintroduced; the industrialists began to make great profits out of re-armament; the Junkers had their privileges confirmed, and the Nazis enriched themselves by plunder and confiscation.

Political Smash and Grab. When Hitler had established his power in Germany he began to carry out his plan for conquering other nations. IT WAS A PLAN WHICH APPEALED TO THE GERMANS. In March, 1938, German troops occupied Austria. In September, 1938, at Munich, the British and French Prime Ministers, who knew their countries were quite unprepared for war, reluctantly agreed to the Nazi annexation of important border areas of Czechoslovakia, where many of the people were of German speech. In March, 1939, the rest of Czechoslovakia was occupied—a flagrant breach of Hitler's promise to Mr. Chamberlain only six months before.

It was now obvious to everyone that Hitler's dreams of conquest knew no bounds. His next victim was to be Poland. Prussia had held parts of Poland for a hundred and fifty years until, in 1918, the Poles at last won back their freedom. Now Hitler resolved to enslave them again. The British and French Governments solemnly warned him that an attack on Poland would bring both countries into the war.

Hitler, drunk with easy successes, did not believe that we would fight. He thought we were too "decadent." On 1st September, 1939, he seized the Free City of Danzig, his armies entered Poland and the Second World War had begun.

WHAT THE NAZIS HAVE DONE TO GERMANY

WHEN Germany is defeated, Hitler and his gang of Nazi leaders will be swept away but it will not be possible to make a clean sweep of the millions of Germans who have at some time worn the Nazi badge. The system will leave a deep mark on German life, and if you are to understand the Germans you must know something of how it worked.

Germany under the Nazis is a "totalitarian state." Hitler is the Dictator, or *"Führer"* (Leader). He not only doubles the parts of president and chancellor; he is supreme law-giver, supreme judge, head of the civil service, commander-in-chief of the armed forces and leader of the Nazi Party. The Cabinet is there merely to advise him; the parliament (*Reichstag*) is there merely to hear his decisions and applaud. His position is more despotic than that of King John in England, before Magna Carta limited his powers more than 700 years ago.

At the head of each of the 15 States into which Germany is divided is one of Hitler's yes-men. These state governors (*Reichs-Statthalter*) appoint the provincial officials; they, on their part, appoint their subordinates and so on down to the smallest employee. No one can be a state or municipal servant in Nazi Germany unless Hitler and Hitler's yes-men are convinced of his loyalty to themselves.

But that is only half the story.

The Nazi Party. Side by side and interlocking with the Nazi Government is the Nazi Party. The Party has its network of officials from the *Gauleiter*, who controls one of the 42 *gaus* into which Germany is divided for purposes of Party organisation, down to the *Blockwart* with the modest job of ruling a block of flats.

Although the same man is often both a government official and a Party official, the functions of the government and the Party are theoretically distinct.

The Party's main concern is to keep the people's faith and enthusiasm for Hitler at boiling point and to turn on the heat for any who are still luke-warm. The function of the government is to carry out Hitler's decrees in practice and run the country on the lines he has laid down.

The national army is, of course, in the service of the government, but the Party has a private army for its own purposes. This Party-army is called the S.A. (STURM-ABTEILUNGEN = STORM TROOPS). But in 1934 there was friction between the S.A. and the regular army and Hitler, who wanted to win the regular army's support, massacred many of the leading S.A. men (including their commander, Captain Röhm).

Hitler's body-guard, THE S.S. (SCHUTZ-STAFFEL = BLACK GUARDS), a more carefully selected and better drilled body of thugs, then took the place of the S.A. as Hitler's personal armed force on the home front.

The notorious GESTAPO (GEHEIME STAATS-POLIZEI = SECRET STATE POLICE), which is responsible for hunting down opponents and killing them or breaking their spirit in concentration camps, is also one of the pillars of Hitler's strength.

All other political parties, and also trade unions, co-operative societies, even boy scout troops and religious organisations for children and young people, were abolished or taken over by the Nazi Party so that no German, man, woman or child, could escape their influence.

When you reach Germany, this evil system will be swept away, but the German people will find it hard to get rid of much of the Nazi creed.

"MEIN KAMPF." Hitler's crude and violent beliefs, few of them original in German thought, are laid down in his book, *Mein Kampf* (My Struggle), which all Germans are supposed to have read.

According to Hitler the State is something above the people. The individual must give up his rights, his liberties, his beliefs, even his religion, for what is held to be the good of the State. But Hitler claims that the Germans are a very special people; they are not only Aryans (by which he apparently meant natives of Northern Europe); they are also the Master Race, and their destiny is to rule and lead all other nations.

The natural enemies of the Master Race are Non-Aryans (Jews), Bolsheviks and Plutocrats. By "Plutocrats" the Nazis generally mean ourselves and the Americans.

Since it is obviously impossible for a Master Race to have been beaten in battle, the Nazis teach that the German

14

armies were not defeated in 1918; Germany would have won, they say, if the Jews, Bolsheviks and other "traitors" inside the country had not "stabbed her in the back."

The Christian virtues of kindness and justice are thought to be unworthy of the Master Race, and the Nazis have tried to uproot them. This involved Hitler in a conflict with the churches. He not only tried to suppress the Protestants and Catholics, but also encouraged the Nazis to invent semi-pagan religions of their own.

It seems strange that such wild ideas could impose on a European nation in the 20th century, but WOVEN INTO HITLER'S DOCTRINE ARE MANY DEEP-SEATED GERMAN "COMPLEXES," SUCH AS HATRED OF THE JEWS, A DESIRE TO DOMINEER OVER OTHERS and a readiness to believe that they themselves are being persecuted.

Who, you may ask, are these Nazis, who go in for such perverted ideas and cruel practices?

In the early days, there were some misled idealists among them, but the leaders are wicked and ambitious men, who have used their power to enrich themselves by plundering first their fellow Germans and then other nations. In this way they have become fabulously wealthy. They stand outside and above German law; they have been answerable for their crimes to no one but Hitler, and he encouraged them.

WHAT THE WAR HAS DONE TO GERMANY

THE Germany you will see is a very different place from the peace-time Germany.

If you come in from the west you will enter the most-bombed area in Europe. Here the destruction is many times greater than anything you have seen in London, Coventry or Bristol. Compare these figures: in eleven months (September, 1940, to July, 1941) the Germans dropped 7,500 tons of bombs on London—we dropped nearly 10,000 tons on Duisburg in two attacks between Saturday morning and Sunday morning, the 14th to 15th October, 1944. In western towns from Hamburg south through the industrial Ruhr and Rhineland—with Essen, Düsseldorf, Duisburg and many other centres—and east to Nuremberg and Munich, you will see areas that consist largely of heaps of rubble and roofless, windowless shells. Cities like Berlin and Hanover in Central Germany will be no better off.

In all these places communal life has been broken up. Mass evacuations have been carried out, not only of children, but of the grown-up population. Only those remained who were needed to staff such factories as could still operate, and to run the civil defence, salvage, police and other essential services. As fast as repairs were made, the R.A.F. blasted them and added to the earlier destruction.

Tens of thousands of Germans have been killed or injured in these raids, hundreds of thousands have lost their belongings and could not replace them because of the short-age of goods.

The Biter Bit. In Western and Central Germany you will find a war area of bleak poverty and devastation. The Germans have been well and truly paid for what they did to Warsaw, Rotterdam and Belgrade.

But the German people have had other things to bear. Probably more than three and a half million German soldiers have been killed in action and another million severely wounded.

The supply of food for German civilians was restricted even before war began so that they could have "guns instead of butter." During the war their rations have been a good deal lower than ours; they have had much less meat, bread and milk and the quality of the food was inferior.

Many of the people you will see in the towns may be under-nourished, though not starving like the people of Poland and Greece.

On top of all this the German workers who remained in industry, and the millions of women who were drafted into the factories, have been worn out by long hours of hard work, which often followed sleepless nights in air-raid shelters. You must therefore expect to find a population that is hungry, exhausted and on the verge of despair.

You will probably find that public services and supplies are working very imperfectly, and it will be urgently necessary to get them going again. Apart from the partial breakdown due to bombing and defeat, the collapse of the Nazi Party will mean that a good deal of routine work is left undone, for in addition to their main task of regimenting their fellow-Germans, the local Nazi officials have done many useful jobs of organisation and relief.

To complete the picture, you are likely to find bands of FOREIGN WORKERS trying to make their way home, mostly men and women WHO WERE CARRIED OFF TO GERMANY AND FORCED TO WORK THERE AS SLAVES OF THE GERMAN WAR-MACHINE. By the end of the war there will be millions of these foreign workers—Russians, French, Poles, Czechs, Belgians, Italians and others—working in Germany. Prisoners of war, of whom Germany has several millions, will also have to be collected from camps, farms and the factories and sent back to their homes.

WHAT THE GERMANS ARE LIKE

When you meet the Germans you will probably think they are very much like us.

They look like us, except that there are fewer of the wiry type and more big, fleshy, fair-haired men and women, especially in the north.

But they are not really so much like us as they look.

The Germans have, of course, many good qualities. They are very hard working and thorough; they are obedient and have a great love of tidiness and order. They are keen on education of a formal sort, and are proud of their "culture" and their appreciation of music, art and literature.

But for centuries they have been trained to submit to authority—not because they thought their rulers wise and right, but because obedience was imposed on them by force.

The old Prussian army—and the Nazi army too—set out intentionally to break the spirit of recruits. They were made to do stupid and humiliating things in order to destroy their self respect and turn them into unquestioning fighting machines. This method produced a formidable military force, but it did not produce good human beings. It made the Germans cringe before authority.

That is one reason why they accepted Hitler. He ordered them about, and most of them liked it. It saved them the trouble of thinking. All they had to do was obey and leave the thinking to him.

It also saved them, they thought, from responsibility. The vile cruelties of the Gestapo and S.S. were nothing to do with them. They did not order them; they did not even want to know about them. The rape of Norway, Holland and Belgium was not their business. It was the business of Hitler and the General Staff.

That is the tale that will be told over and over again by the Germans. They will protest with deep sincerity that they are as innocent as a babe in arms.

BUT THE GERMAN PEOPLE CANNOT SLIDE OUT OF THEIR RESPONSIBILITY QUITE SO EASILY. You must remember that

Hitler became Chancellor in a strictly legal way. Nearly half the German electors voted for him in the last (comparatively) free election of 1933. With the votes of his Nationalist allies he had a clear majority. The Germans knew what he stood for —it was in his book—and they approved it. Hitler was immensely popular with the majority of Germans: they regarded him as the restorer of German greatness. They welcomed the abolition of unemployment although they knew that it arose from conscription and rearmament. AFTER THE FALL OF FRANCE MOST GERMANS SUPPORTED HIS MILITARY CONQUESTS WITH ENTHUSIASM. IT WAS ONLY WHEN THEY FELT THE COLD WIND OF DEFEAT THAT THEY DISCOVERED THEIR CONSCIENCES.

The Mind of the German. The Germans adore military show. In Nazi Germany everyone has a uniform. If it isn't the uniform of the Army, Navy or Air Force, it is that of the S.A., S.S. or some other Party organisation. Even the little boys and girls have been strutting about in the uniform of the Hitler Youth or the Union of German Girls.

Such uniforms may still impress the Germans, but they will not impress you. But you must do justice to the position of the ordinary German policeman. He will have no authority over British troops, but you should do nothing to make more difficult any task he may be allotted by the Allies.

THE UNIFORMS YOU WILL RESPECT ARE THOSE OF THE BRITISH AND ALLIED FORCES.

It is important that you should BE SMART AND SOLDIERLY in appearance and behaviour. The Germans think nothing of a slovenly soldier.

You will run across Germans who are genuinely ashamed of being Germans. Even before Hitler made Germany universally hated, they had a sense of national inferiority. They felt that other nations, like the British, Americans and French, were somehow ahead of them. There is little doubt that Hitler realised this, and used his theory of the Master Race to overcome it. He tried to make the Germans think well of themselves, and he overdid it. There will be some—especially the young ones—who have swallowed the tale that they are members of the Master Race, and are therefore our superiors.

There is no need to say much more about German brutality; it has been unmistakably revealed in the Nazi methods of governing and of waging war. But you may think it strange that the Germans are at the same time sentimental. They love melancholy songs; they easily get sorry for themselves; even childless old couples insist on having their Christmas tree. German soldiers would play with Polish or Russian children, and yet there are enough authentic reports of these same children being shot or burnt or starved to death.

This mixture of sentimentality and callousness does not show a well-balanced mind. The Germans are not good at controlling their feelings. They have a streak of hysteria. You will find that Germans may often fly into a passion if some little thing goes wrong.

How Hitler moulded them. Hitler set to work, for his own purposes, to cultivate these weaknesses and vices of the German character.

He wanted his Nazis to be still more brutal because he thought that in this way he could terrify the German nation, and other nations too, into submission. Tens of thousands of young men in the S.S. have been systematically trained as torturers and executioners. Some went mad in the process, but others reached a point where they can commit any atrocity with indifference or even with pleasure.

Ordinary members of the public have been taught to spy on each other. Little boys and girls in the Hitler Youth have been encouraged to denounce their parents and teachers if they let slip some incautious criticism of Hitler or his government. The result is that no one in Nazi Germany can trust his fellows, friendship and family affection have been undermined, and thousands of anti-Nazi Germans have been forced to pretend—even in their own homes—that they admire the men and principles which in their hearts they despise. Lying and hypocrisy became a necessity.

Hitler's own breaches of faith—especially in his dealings with other nations—were represented as skilful diplomacy. The Germans admired his success and came to admire his methods.

Worst of all, perhaps, it has been drummed into German children in the schools and Hitler Youth that might is right, war the finest form of human activity and Christianity just slushy sentiment. By cramming children's minds with Nazi ideas and preventing any other ideas from reaching them, Hitler hoped to breed a race of robots after his own heart. We cannot yet judge to what extent this inhuman plan has succeeded.

So you will not be surprised if the German proves to be less like us than he appears at first sight.

This does not mean that all Germans are liars, hypocrites and brutes. Even Nazi methods of education have not been so successful as all that; but it does mean that the national character of the Germans has worsened a good deal under Nazi influence.

Be on your Guard. When you deal with Germans you must be on your guard. We were taken in by them after the last war: many of us swallowed their story about the "cruel" Treaty of Versailles, although it was really far more lenient than the terms they themselves had imposed on Russia only a year before; many of us believed their talk about disarmament and the sincerity of their desire for peace. And so we let ourselves in for this war, which has been a good deal bigger than the last. There are signs that the German leaders are already making plans for a Third World War. That must be prevented at all costs.

When you get to Germany it is possible that some civilians will welcome your arrival, and may even look on you as their liberators from Hitler's tyranny. These will be among the

Germans who consistently opposed Hitler during his years of success. Not that they made speeches against him or committed sabotage: any who did that are unlikely to be alive to welcome you. But there are many who kept their own counsel and passively opposed Hitler all along.

As a rule they are loyal members of the political parties suppressed by Hitler, mostly workers, but often honest people of the middle classes. Or they are Catholics or Protestants, who have opposed Hitler because of his persecution of Christianity.

But many Germans will pretend they have been anti-Nazis simply because they want to be on the winning side. Among them will be many doubtful characters. Even those who seem to have the best intentions cannot be regarded as trustworthy; they are almost certain to have some axe to grind. That is one of the reasons why you have been instructed not to fraternise with the Germans.

There are fanatical young Nazis—girls as well as boys—whose heads and hearts are still full of the vicious teachings they absorbed in the Hitler Youth. Their talk, if you ever heard it, might sound plausible and even rather fine, for Hitler's propagandists have naturally dressed up his ideas to make them attractive to the young. But remember that the real meaning of Nazism is shown in its vile practices, not in its fair words.

And, quite possibly, you will some day run into one of the genuine thugs, one of the former killers or crooked Nazi bosses. He may try to throw his weight about, or he may cringe and try to curry favour. Such people really respect nothing but force.

The authorities will know how to deal with them.

WHAT THE GERMANS THINK OF US

IF we leave the extreme Nazi ideas out of account, the basic German view of the British is something like this:

The British do not work so hard as the Germans or take their work so seriously.

The British do not organise as well as the Germans. (In fact the German tends to over-organise; this war has shown that our organisation, when we really get down to it, is just as thorough and more flexible.)

But on the whole the Germans admire the British. The efforts of the German Propaganda Ministry to stir up hatred against us have not been, in spite of the R.A.F. raids, a great success. It is probable that of all the occupying troops of the United Nations we and the Americans will be the least unwelcome.

Even Hitler had a grudging respect for us, as he admitted in *Mein Kampf*. He envied us the British Empire and admired the national qualities that went to building it up—imagination, enterprise and tough endurance. He thought we had grown decadent and lost them. Our fighting forces—and the civilians at home—have proved the contrary.

25

Germans believe we have other national virtues. They think that we are fair, decent and tolerant and that we have political common sense.

Now that the Nazi dream of world-conquest has been shattered, these homely qualities look all the more attractive, and many Germans would probably say to-day that their ideal of the new Germany is something like Britain.

WHILE YOU ARE SERVING IN GERMANY YOU ARE REPRESENTATIVES OF BRITAIN. Your behaviour will decide their opinion of us.

It is not that we value their opinion for its own sake. It is good for the Germans, however, to see that soldiers of the British democracy are self-controlled and self-respecting, that in dealing with a conquered nation they can be firm, fair and decent. The Germans will have to become fair and decent themselves, if we are to live with them in peace later on.

But the Germans have another pet idea. They claim that we are nationally akin to them, they call us their "cousins." This is part of their theory of the superiority of the Northern races.

The likeness, if it exists at all, is only skin-deep. THE DEEPER YOU DIG INTO THE GERMAN CHARACTER, THE MORE YOU REALISE HOW DIFFERENT THEY ARE FROM US. SO DON'T BE TAKEN IN BY FIRST IMPRESSIONS.

The Germans think of the Americans much in the same way as they think of us, but they do not know them so well and many of their ideas come from Hollywood films, which were once very popular in Germany. That is why they think, for instance, that all Americans are rich. Their first idea of the American troops as "amateur" soldiers has been completely disproved by battle experience.

The Germans' attitude to the Russians is quite different. Under Hitler they have been taught to regard the Russians as sub-human. The purpose of this was to remove any scruples they might have had about the barbarous methods of German warfare on the Russian front. The Soviet citizen, Hitler said, was less than a human being, so no treatment could be too cruel for him. The "Bolsheviks" were bracketed with the Jews as Enemy of Mankind No. 1.

When the Red Army began to advance Hitler redoubled this propaganda. He hoped to frighten his troops and the civilians at home into resistance to the death. And to some extent he succeeded.

The severity of the Red Army's fight for liberation is easy to understand. HITLER, RUNNING TRUE TO FORM, ATTACKED RUSSIA WHILE THE PACT OF FRIENDSHIP HE HAD MADE WITH HER WAS STILL IN FORCE; he has spurred on his soldiers and S.S. to commit atrocities more barbarous than anything in modern history—except their own record in Poland.

Ever since the Germans invaded Russia in 1941, their propaganda has been spreading baseless scares about the "Bolshevik menace." The aim was perfectly clear—it was to drive a wedge between us and our Russian ally. Remember this if the Germans try to spread stories against the Red Army.

HOW THE GERMANS LIVE

THE INSTRUCTIONS YOU WILL RECEIVE IN GERMANY WILL KEEP YOU VERY MUCH APART FROM THE GERMANS. Probably you will rarely, if ever, enter a house where Germans are living, and neither will you be meeting Germans on social occasions; but you should know something of how they live so as to understand what is going on around you.

Life in any country of Central or Western Europe is not—under peace-time conditions—very different from what it is at home, but there are quite a lot of smaller differences. For instance there is—

Food. Probably you will seldom come across food cooked in the German way. Even if you do, it may be very different from pre-war German food. It is likely to be a long time before German supplies get back to normal.

At its best, German cooking produces some characteristic and appetising dishes. The chief difference from English cooking is in the treatment of vegetables. In place of the English boiled greens the Germans serve a white pickled cabbage called *Sauerkohl* (sour cabbage) or a red cabbage called *Rotkohl*. Both are very tasty if you eat them with *Wiener Schnitzel* (fried veal) or *Schweine-kotelett* (fried pork cutlet).

The Germans prefer pork and veal to beef and mutton, and cook them better. But the staple meat dish is the sausage. The best German sausage is eaten cold and there are hundreds of varieties of it. Two excellent kinds of sausage are *Mettwurst* (Wurst = sausage) and *Leberwurst* (liver sausage).

The Germans are very fond of *Torten* (pastries), with *Schlagsahne* (whipped cream), but it will be some time before such luxuries are obtainable again at the *Konditorei* (confectioner's). The Germans don't know how to make tea, but they are quite expert with coffee. However, for the present their coffee is "*ersatz.*"

"Beer is best." The favourite German drink is beer. Under war conditions it has been diluted much more even than English beer, but normally it is regarded as the pleasantest beer in Europe. There are hundreds of brews; two of the most famous are Münchener (from Munich) and Pilsener (from Pilsen in Czechoslovakia). Local beers are either light (*hell*) or dark (*dunkel*). All German beers are iced.

Western Germany produces some of the choicest wine on the Continent, such as Moselle wine and Rhine wine (which we call "hock"). Compared with prices in Britain wine is cheap.

Whiskey and gin will be scarce and of poor quality (unless imported from Britain), BUT THERE ARE MANY KINDS OF SPIRITS CALLED SCHNAPS. THE CHEAPER SORTS ARE GUARANTEED TO TAKE THE SKIN OFF ONE'S THROAT.

Entertainment. Entertainment will be provided for you by E.N.S.A. in your own camp or barracks and most German places of entertainment will be out of bounds. The Germans, of course, will be going to cinemas where it is probable that British, American and Russian films will be shown. There may also be German films—non-political ones. But German films, which were very good before 1933, suffered like so many other things because Hitler insisted on making them an instrument of Nazi propaganda, and there may at first be very few available which are free from this taint. This is also true of German plays.

Sport. The Germans have only taken to sport during the last thirty years, but they are keen and capable performers. They learnt most of their sport from us. Football is the most popular game, but is played less vigorously than in Britain; charging is regarded as rough play. Football is entirely amateur, and "pools" are unknown. There is no cricket, but plenty of athletics, some tennis and a little golf. Boxing and wrestling are both popular spectacles, and the Germans go in for a good deal of cycle racing.

Health. The standards of health, normally high, have fallen as a result of the war. Venereal diseases are prevalent. A GERMAN EXPERT STATED (MAY, 1943), "VENEREAL DISEASES STRIKE AT EVERY FOURTH PERSON BETWEEN THE AGES OF 15 AND 41."

Women. Before Hitler came to power the German woman

was winning the same freedom to live her own life as British women enjoy, but the Nazis took away her newly won rights and made her again the traditional *Hausfrau* (housewife). Shortage of man-power in war time brought German women back into the professions, but only on sufferance.

Under the shock of defeat standards of personal honour, already undermined by the Nazis, will sink still lower. Numbers of German women will be willing, if they can get the chance, to make themselves cheap for what they can get out of you. After the last war prostitutes streamed into the zone occupied by British and American troops. They will probably try this again, even though this time you will be living apart from the Germans. Be on your guard. Most of them will be infected.

MARRIAGES BETWEEN MEMBERS OF BRITISH FORCES AND GERMANS ARE, AS YOU KNOW, FORBIDDEN.

But for this prohibition such marriages would certainly take place. Germany will not be a pleasant place to live in for some time after the war, and German girls know that, if they marry British husbands, they will become British with all the advantages of belonging to a victor nation instead of to a vanquished one. Many German girls will be just waiting for the chance to marry a Briton—whether they care for him or not. When once they had their marriage lines he would have served his purpose.

During the last occupation there were a number of marriages between British soldiers and German girls. The great

majority of these marriages soon came to grief. When the couples returned to England they found themselves lonely and friendless, and this resulted only in unhappiness for the wife, the husband and the children. That is one reason—though not the only one—why this time they will not be allowed.

Religion. Large parts of Germany have been Protestant since the Reformation in the early 16th century, when Martin Luther led the revolt against the papacy. To-day about two-thirds of Germany is Protestant and one-third Catholic; the Protestants are strongest in North and Central Germany, the Catholics in the west, south and south-east.

Many of the Catholic churches are of great beauty and antiquity. Some, like Cologne Cathedral, have unfortunately suffered in raids, but there are many other noble and ancient churches which are well worth seeing. A few of the most famous are: in Central Germany, the cathedrals of Naumburg and Hildesheim; in South Germany those of Speyer, Bamberg and Worms.

Music. The Germans are extremely fond of music and have produced composers and performers of great eminence. Beethoven, Bach, Brahms, Wagner were all Germans. There are fine concerts of classical music in most of the larger German towns.

Jazz and Swing are frowned on by the Nazis because they

are not considered Nordic, but the Germans are fond of dancing, and some dance bands are still playing the latest American and British hits.

Literature. Many of the best German writers had opposed Hitler before his advent to power or had expressed a view of life contrary to Fascism. Their books were therefore banned in Germany and copies of many of them publicly burnt. Jewish writers, some of whom had been in the front rank, were also banned. It has been difficult for a writer to earn a living in Germany unless he was willing to use his talents to spread Nazi ideas. So if you know German and wish to read German books you will find few that are not tainted by Hitler-propaganda, unless they were written by anti-Nazi refugees and published abroad.

For the same reasons, modern painters and scientists of independent thought have been silenced or forced to escape from the great intellectual prison of Hitler-Germany.

It will take a long time for Germany to reach again the high level she had attained in the things of the mind under the free republic that preceded Hitler.

General. The rule of the road is: Keep to the Right—not to the Left as in Britain.

In Germany every town and village has a mayor (*Bürgermeister*); if it is a town with a population of over 20,000 he is probably called an *Oberbürgermeister*. But whatever his title, he has essential administrative duties to perform and is a more important official than his opposite number in England.

IF YOU HAVE TO GIVE ORDERS TO GERMAN CIVILIANS, GIVE THEM IN A FIRM, MILITARY MANNER. THE GERMAN CIVILIAN IS USED TO IT AND EXPECTS IT.

The Germans are very short of clothes and foot-wear. Look out for attempts to steal, beg or buy your boots, shirts and underclothes. You don't need to be told that it is a serious offence to sell or give away Government property.

IF YOU SHOULD BE BILLETED IN A GERMAN HOUSE-HOLD—THOUGH THIS WILL VERY SELDOM HAPPEN—BE COURTEOUS BUT ALOOF, AVOID LOOSE TALK AND LOOSE CON-DUCT, AND KEEP YOUR EYES AND EARS OPEN.

With their habitual reverence for all things military, the Germans will be quick to notice any slackness in the dress or bearing of British troops. Don't let your Country or your Unit down.

It is only natural that Germans who have suffered personally under Nazi oppression will try to take revenge on their local tyrants. They will regard this as their own affair and will resent interference. Don't go looking for trouble.

THE NAZIS HAVE HAD GREAT EXPERIENCE IN ORGANISING INCIDENTS TO CAUSE TROUBLE OR TO INFLUENCE PUBLIC OPINION. The die-hards (mostly young products of the Hitler Youth) may try to play similar tricks even when their country has been occupied. IF THE INCIDENT IS SMALL, KEEP YOUR HEAD AND REFUSE TO BE IMPRESSED OR PUT OUT

OF COUNTENANCE. IF IT IS BIG, THE ALLIED AUTHORITIES WILL DEAL WITH IT.

As soon as the pressure of Hitlerism is removed, political parties will spring up again. Even if they have names similar to our parties they will have different problems and different aims. STEER CLEAR OF ANYTHING CONNECTED WITH GERMAN POLITICS.

MONEY

THE smallest German coin is the Pfennig. 100 Pfennigs make one Mark or more formally "Reichsmark."

When you enter Germany you will be given official information about the number of Marks which go to the £.

German coins at present in circulation are: —

1, 5, and 10 Pfennig pieces, made of zinc, 5 and 10 Pfennig pieces made of an aluminium-bronze alloy, an aluminium 50 Pfennig piece, and 2 Mark and 5 Mark pieces of a silver-copper alloy.

In addition to these coins you may come across the following notes: 1, 2 and 5 Mark notes issued by the Rentenbank, and 10, 20, 50, 100 and 1,000 Mark notes issued by the Reichsbank.

WHEREVER YOU ARE STATIONED IN GERMANY YOU WILL FIND AT FIRST THAT THERE IS PRACTICALLY NOTHING TO BUY. Food, clothing and tobacco will be severely rationed; there will be no little things you can send home as gifts; the shops will be empty. YOUR NEEDS WILL BE LOOKED AFTER BY NAVY, ARMY AND R.A.F. ISSUE AND THE NAAFI STORES. The only thing you can buy from the Germans will be a glass of beer or wine.

It will be a long time before the basic needs of the German population are satisfied and inessential goods are again produced.

So for the time being there is little you can do with your pay except save it. You should therefore draw the minimum.

MAKING YOURSELF UNDERSTOOD

ENGLISH is taught in all German secondary schools and is a compulsory subject in most; it is also taught in large numbers of commercial and language schools throughout the country, so that many Germans have at least a smattering of English. In any hotel or larger restaurant, or government or municipal office, or large shop, there will almost certainly be someone who speaks English.

But in the depths of the country or in working-class districts, you may have to speak German if you cannot get through with the language of signs.

Many German words are similar to English, especially those in most common use. For instance, *Mann* = man, *Haus* = house, *Garten* = garden, *butter* = butter, and *Brot* = bread. This is because the two languages have grown largely from the same root.

A list of words and phrases is printed at the end of this book, and indications are given of how to pronounce them.

The pronunciation is straightforward except for two or three German sounds which we do not use in English.

The golden rule in trying to speak a language you do not know is to be as simple as possible. Take a two-year-old child as our model. Don't try to make sentences; use nouns and verbs.

At the beginning try to ask questions which can be answered by *Ja* (yes) or *Nein* (no). Speak in a normal voice; you will not make your meaning any clearer by shouting.

If you are not understood, point to the word or sentence in your list of phrases.

DO'S

REMEMBER you are a representative of the British Commonwealth.

KEEP your eyes and ears open.

BE SMART and soldierly in dress and bearing.

AVOID loose talk and loose conduct.

BE FIRM AND FAIR in any dealings with Germans.

KEEP GERMANS AT A DISTANCE, even those with whom you have official dealings.

STEER CLEAR of all disputes between German political parties.

GO EASY on Schnaps.

REMEMBER that in Germany "venereal diseases strike at every fourth person between the ages of 15 and 41."

40

DON'TS

DON'T sell or give away dress or equipment.

DON'T be sentimental. If things are tough for the Germans they have only themselves to blame. They made things much worse for the innocent people of the countries they occupied.

DON'T believe German accounts of the war or the events that led up to it. The Germans got their ideas on these subjects from lying propaganda.

DON'T fall for political hard-luck stories.

DON'T believe tales against our Allies or the Dominions. They are aimed at sowing ill will between us.

DON'T be taken in by surface resemblances between the Germans and ourselves.

DON'T go looking for trouble.

WORDS AND PHRASES

Note on Pronunciation

IN German, the letters of the alphabet are pronounced differently from what they are in English. Therefore under each German word in the following list is an English spelling which reproduces as nearly as possible the sound of the German. It does not always give the sound of the German quite correctly, because there are a few sounds in German which do not exist in English at all and therefore there is no English way of spelling them. In such cases the English spelling has been chosen which comes nearest to the German sound. If you speak plainly, your meaning should be quite clear, and that is all that matters at this stage.

Note the following points about this English spelling of German sounds:—

1. The syllables printed in italics are those on which the accent falls. E.g. *fah*ter (father), zol*dah*ten (soldiers).

2. Where a hyphen (-) is inserted, there is a natural break in the word. E.g. *vy*ter-*fah*ren (drive on), *fahr-raht* (bicycle).

3. The *g* sound is always like *g* in GO, and never like *g* in GEORGE.

4. The *ow* sound is always like *ow* in HOW.

5. The *y* sound is always as in MY and not as in CITY.

6. The *r* should be pronounced, except in the sound *ur*.

Orders

Hands up!	**Hände hoch!**
	*hend*a hohk
Open your hands!	**Öffnen Sie die Hände!**
	*uff*nen zee dee *hend*a
Halt! Who goes there?	**Halt! Wer da?**
	hahlt vair dah
Give me your papers.	**Geben Sie mir Ihre Papiere**
	*gay*ben zee meer eera pa*peera*
Sit down!	**Setzen Sie sich!**
	*zet*sen zee zish
Stand up!	**Stehen Sie auf**
	*shtay*en zee owf

General

Yes, No	**Ja, Nein**
	yah, nine
Please, Thank you.	**Bitte, Danke**
	*bitt*a, *dahnk*a
Thank you very much	**Danke sehr**
	*dahnk*a zair
Good morning (day, evening) . .	**Guten Morgen (Tag, Abend)**
	*goot*en *mor*gen (tahk *ah*bent)
Mr., Mrs., Miss.	**Herr, Frau, Fräulein**
	hair, frow, *froy*line
Man, woman, child	**Mann, Frau, Kind**
	mahn, frow, kinnt
Father, mother, brother, sister .	**Vater, Mutter, Bruder, Schwester**
	*fah*ter, *moo*ter, *broo*der, *shves*ter

43

Husband, wife, son, daughter, fiancée	**Mann, Frau, Sohn, Tochter, Braut**
	mahn, frow, zohn, *tohk*ter, browt
I, you, she, he, we, they	**Ich, Sie, sie, er, wir, sie**
	ish, zee, zee, air, veer, zee
My, his, her, our, your, their	**Mein, sein, ihr, unser, Ihr, ihr**
	mine, zine, eer, *oon*ser, eer, eer
Excuse me	**Entschuldigen Sie**
	ent*shool*diggen zee
I beg your pardon	**Verzeihung**
	fair*tsy*oong
Is there anyone who speaks English?	**Spricht jemand englisch?**
	shprisht *yay*mant *eng*lish
Please write (read) this	**Bitte schreiben Sie (lesen Sie) das**
	*Bitt*a *shry*ben zee (*lay*zen zee) dass
Who are you?	**Wer sind Sie?**
	vair zint zee
What is your name?	**Wie heissen Sie?**
	vee *hy*ssen zee
Where do you live?	**Wo wohnen Sie?**
	vo *voh*nen zee
Please bring me—	**Bitte bringen Sie mir—**
	*bitt*a *bring*en zee meer—
give me—.	**geben Sie mir—**
	*gay*ben zee meer—
lend me—.	**leihen Sie mir—**
	*ly*en zee meer
Borrow, exchange, receipt	**Borgen, tauschen, Quittung**
	*borg*en, *tow*shen, *qvit*oong
Have you—? How much?	**Haben Sie, —Wie viel?**
	*hah*ben zee—, vee feel?

44

I am glad, I am sorry	**Es freut mich, es tut mir leid**
	es froyt mish, es toot meer lite
I like this very much	**Ich habe das sehr gern**
	ish *hah*ba das zair gairn
Come in!	**Herein!**
	hair*ine*!
Quick, slowly	**Schnell, langsam**
	shnell, *lank*sahm
It is late (early).	**Es ist spät, (früh)**
	es ist shpate, (free)
I am in a hurry.	**Ich habe es eilig**
	ish *hah*ba es *eye*lish
Take care!.	**Achtung! or Vorsicht!**
	*ahk*toong! *fore*zisht!
Wait here, please	**Warten Sie hier, bitte**
	*vahr*ten zee here *bitt*a
We are friends	**Wir sind Freunde**
	veer zint *froyn*da
Don't be afraid.	**Keine Angst**
	*ky*na angst
I will return later.	**Ich komme später zurück**
	ish *komm*a *shpate*r tsoo*rick*
I will meet you here at ... o'clock	**Ich treffe Sie Hier um ... Uhr**
	ish *treff*a zee here oom ... oor
Why, when, where	**Warum? Wann? Wo?**
	vah*room*? vahn? vo?
What do you call this?	**Wie heisst dies?**
	vee *hy*st dees?
What does that mean?.	**Was bedeutet das?**
	vahss be*doyt*et dass?
Say it again	**Wiederholen Sie es**
	veeder*hohl*en zee ess

I don't understand	**Ich verstehe nicht**
	ish fair*shtay*a nisht
Do you understand?	**Verstehen Sie?**
	fair*shtay*en zee?
Please speak slowly	**Bitte sprechen Sie langsam**
(write it down).	**(schreiben Sie es auf)**
	*bitt*a shpreshen zee *lank*sahm
	(*shry*ben zee ess owf)
What do you want?	**Was wollen Sie?**
	vahss *voll*en zee?
What is the matter?	**Was ist los?**
	vahss ist lohs?
What is the time?	**Wie spät ist es?**
	vee shpate ist ess?
Where are you going?	**Wo gehen sie [*sic*] hin?**
	vo *gay*en zee hin?
I need—	**Ich brauche—**
	ish *brow*ka—
I have lost—.	**Ich have [*sic*]—verloren**
	ish *hah*ba—fair*loh*ren
What nationality are you?	**Was für ein Landsmann sind Sie?**
	vahss feer ine *lants*mahn zint zee?
Are you German (French)?.	**Sind Sie Deutscher (Franzose)?**
	zint zee *doy*cher (frahn*tsohz*a)?
What is the name of this town (this village)?	**Wie heisst diese Stadt (dieses Dorf)?**
	vee hyst *dee*za shtat (*dee*zes dorf)?
Have you seen any soldiers?	**Haben Sie Soldaten gesehen?**
	*hab*ben zee zol*dah*ten ge*zayn*?
What kind of soldiers?	**Was für Soldaten?**
	vahss feer zol*dah*ten?

46

Where is the town-hall? . . . . (police-station)	**Wo ist das Rathaus (Polizeiamt)?** vo ist dass *raht*house (pollit*s*yamt)?
That is wrong	**Das ist falsch** dass ist falsh
Go away, please	**Bitte gehen Sie weg** *bitt*a *gay*en zee veck
I cannot talk to you now . . .	**Ich kann jetzt nicht mit Ihnen sprechen** ish khan yetst nisht mit *ee*nen *shpresh*en
I know nothing about it	**Ich weiss nichts davon** ish vice nishts da*fon*

Travelling by Road

Is this the way to—?	**Führt dieser Weg nach—?** feert *dee*zer vaik nahk—?
Which is the way to—?	**Wie kommt man nach—?** vee kommt mahn nahk—?
How far is it to—?	**Wie weit ist es nach—?** vee vite ist ess nahk—?
Where does this road lead to? . . .	**Wohin führt diese Strasse?** vo*hin* feert *dee*za *shtrah*ssa?
Where am I now? Show me on this map	**Wo bin ich jetzt? Zeigen Sie es mir auf diesem Plan** vo bin ish yetzt? *tsy*gen zee ess meer owf *dee*zem plahn
Straight on	**Geradeaus** ge*rah*da-owss
Turn to the left (right)	**Biegen Sie links (rechts) um** *bee*gen zee links (reshts) oom

47

Is this road clear of obstructions? .	**Ist diese Strasse frei von Hindernissen?**
	ist *deeza shtrah*ssa fry fon *hin*dernissen?
I have lost my way	**Ich habe den Weg verloren**
	ish *hah*ba dain vaik fair*loh*ren
I want to go (back) to—	**Ich will nach—(zurück)**
	ish vill nahk—(tsoo*rick*)
Can I park here?	**Kann ich hier parken?**
	kahn ish here *pahr*ken?
Stop! Go back!.	**Stopp! Zurück!**
	shtop! tsoo*rick*!
Go on!	**Weiterfahren!**
	*vy*ter-*fah*ren!
Danger!	**Achtung, Gefahr!**
	*ahk*toong, ge*fahr*!
Main road, good road, ... secondary road, track	**Chaussee, gute Strasse, Nebenstrasse, Fahrweg**
	sho*say*, *goo*ta *shtrah*ssa, *nay*ben-*shtrah*ssa, *fahr*vaik
Road closed. No thoroughfare . .	**Gesperrt. Kein Durchgang**
	ge*shpairt*. kine *doorsh*gang
One-way street (traffic)	**Einbahnstrasse (-verkehr)**
	*ine*bahn-*shtrah*ssa (-fair*kair*)
Cross road. Level crossing . . .	**Kreuzung, Bahnübergang**
	*kroyt*zoong, *bah*neebergang
Keep to the left (right)	**Links (rechts) fahren**
	links (reshts) *fah*ren
Bicycle, horse, mule, cart . . .	**Fahrrad, Pferd, Maultier, Wagen**
	fahr-raht, pfairt, *mowl*teer, *vah*gen

Car Repairs

My car (lorry) has broken down. . **Mein Wagen (Lastwagen) hat eine Panne gehabt**
mine *vah*gen (*last*vahgen) haht *eye*na *pann*a ge*hah*bt

Where is the nearest garage? . . . **Wo ist die nächste Garage?**
vo ist dee *naiksta* ga*rah*ja?

Can you repair (replace) this?. . . **Können Sie das reparieren (auswechseln)?**
*kenn*en zee dass repp*areer*en (*owssvex*eln)

Can you fetch (tow) my car? . . . **Können Sie meinen Wagen holen (abschleppen)?**
*kenn*en zee *my*nen *vah*gen *hoh*len (*ap-shlepp*en)?

I need petrol (oil, water) . . . . . **Ich brauche Benzin (Oel, Wasser)**
ish *brow*ka bent*seen* (ull, *vahss*er)

Can you lend me some tools? . . . **Können Sie mir Werkzeuge leihen?**
*kenn*en zee meer *vairk*tsoyga *ly*en?

Travelling by Rail

Where is the railway station? . . . **Wo ist der Bahnhof?**
vo ist dair *bahn*hof?

When is there a train to—? . . . . **Wann fährt ein Zug nach—?**
vahn fairt ine tsook nahk—?

What time does it arrive? . . . . **Wann kommt er an?**
vahn kommt air an?

49

Do I have to change?	**Muss ich umsteigen?**
	mooss *ish oom*shtygen?
A single (return) ticket to— . . .	**Eine Fahrkarte (Rückfahrkarte)**
	nach—
	*eye*na *fahr*karta (*rick*fahrkarta)
	nahk—
Ticket office	**Fahrkartenausgabe**
	*fahr*karten-owssgahba
Refreshment room	**Bahnhofrestaurant**
	*bahn*hof-resto*rong*

The Town

Mayor, parson, police	**Bürgermeister, Pfarrer, Polizei**
	*beerger-my*ster, *pfarr*er, pollit*sy*
Town-hall, church, ...	**Rathaus, Kirche,**
police station, fire-station	**Polizeiamt, Feuerwache**
	*raht*house, *keer*sha, pollit*syamt*,
	*foyer*vakka
Hospital, power-station	**Krankenhaus, Kraftwerk**
	*krank*enhouse, *krafft*vairk
When is the museum	**Wann wird das Museum**
(picture-gallery) open?	**(die Bildergallerie) geöffnet?**
	vahn veert dass moo*zay*oom
	(dee *bill*der-galle*ree*) ge-*eff*net?
Where is the factory	**Wo ist die Fabrik**
(harbour, aerodrome)?	**(der Hafen, der Flugplatz)?**
	vo ist dee fab*reek*
	(dair *hah*fen, dair *floog*plats)?

50

The Country, the Sea

Bridge, ford, river . . . . . . **Brücke, Furt, Fluss**
*brick*a, foort, flooss

Mountain, forest, wood, canal . . **Berg, Forst, Wald, Kanal**
bairg, forst, vahlt, kan*ahl*

Farm. . . . . **Bauernhof**
*bow*ern-hof

Are the trees in that wood thick? . **Stehen die Bäume dicht in**
 diesem Wald?
*shtay*en dee *boy*ma disht in
 *deez*em vahlt?

Field, ploughed field, pasture . . **Feld, Acker, Wiese**
felt, *ack*er, *vee*za

Whose cattle (horses) are these?. . **Wem gehören dieses Vieh**
 (diese Pferde)?
vaim ge*hur*en *deez*es fee
 (*deeza pfair*da)?

Can we sleep in your barn . . . . **Können wir in Ihrer Scheune**
 (out-buildings)? **(Anbau) shlafen [sic]?**
*kenn*en veer [in] *eer*er *shoy*na
 (*ahn*bow) *shlah*fen?

Fodder, hay, straw, wheat, crops. . **Futter, Heu, Stroh, Korn, Ernte**
*foot*er, hoy, shtroh, korrn, *airn*ta

Horse, cow, sheep, goat, chicken, . **Pferd, Kuh, Schaf, Ziege, Huhn,**
 goose **Gans**
pfairt, koo, shahf, *tsee*ga, hoon,
 gahnss

Is there a spring (well, stream) . . **Gibt es eine Quelle (einen Brun-**
 near here? **nen, ein Bach) in der Nähe?**
geebt ess *eye*na *kvell*a (*eye*nen
 *broo*nen, ine bahk) in dair *nay*a?

51

Sea, quay, island	**Meer, Quai, Insel**
	mayr, ky, *in*zel
Boat, rowing boat, sail	**Boot, Ruderboot, Segel**
	boat, *roo*der-boat, *zay*gel
High tide, low tide, current, wind .	**Flut, Ebbe, Strömung, Wind**
	floot, *ebb*a, *shtree*moong, vinnt

Accommodation, Baths

Where can I get a bed?	**Wo kann ich shlafen** [*sic*] **?**
	vo kahn ish *shlah*fen?
These are my (our) billets	**Ich bin (wir sind) hier ein-quartiert**
	ish bin (veer zint) here *ine*-kvarteert
May I (we) come in?	**Darf ich (dürfen wir) eintreten?**
	darf ish (*deer*fen veer) *ine*-trayten?
I shall be returning late (leaving early)	**Ich komme spät zurück (gehe früh fort)**
	ish *komm*a shpate tsoo*rick* (*gay*a free fort)
Can we have something to eat (drink)?	**Können wir etwas zu essen (trinken) bekommen?**
	*kenn*en veer *et*vahss tsoo *ess*en (*trink*en) be*komm*en?
May I have a key?	**Kann ich einen Schlüssel haben?**
	kahn ish *eye*nen *shliss*el *hah*ben?
Where is the light?	**Wo ist das Licht?**
	vo ist dass lisht?

A hot bath, soap, towel	**Ein warmes Bad, Seife, Handtuch**
	ine *vahr*mes baht, *z*yfa, *hahnt*-toohk
Lavatory, cloakroom, dining room	**Abort, Garderobe, Esszimmer**
	*ahp*ort, *gar*da-*roh*ba, *ess*tsimmer

Food, Drink

Where can I eat (drink)?	**Wo kann ich essen (trinken)?**
	vo kahn ish *essen* (*trin*ken)?
May I have breakfast (supper, dinner)?	**Kann ich Frühstück (Mittagessen, Abendbrot) haben?**
	kahn ish *free*shtick (*mitt*ahk-essen, *ah*bent-broht) *hah*ben?
Menu, bottle, cup, glass, jug . . .	**Speisekarte, Flasche, Tasse, Glas, Krug**
	*shpy*za-karta, *flash*a, *tahss*a, glahss, krook
Knife, fork, plate, spoon	**Messer, Gabel, Teller, Löffel**
	*mess*er, *gah*bel, *tell*er, *leff*el
Bread, butter, cheese, eggs	**Brot, Butter, Käse, Eier**
	broht, *boot*er, *kay*za, *eye*r
Fish, meat, vegetables.	**Fisch, Fleisch, Gemüse**
	fish, flysh, ge*mee*za
The butcher (greengrocer). . . .	**Der Fleischer (Gemüsehändler)**
	dair *fly*sher (ge*mee*za-*hendl*er)
The fruiterer, apples, pears, plums	**Der Obsthändler, Äpfel, Birnen, Pflaumen**
	dair *obst*-hendler, *ep*fel, *beer*nen, *pflow*men

53

How much a pound (kilo, liter) . .	**Was kostet das Pfund, (Kilo, Liter)?**
	vahss kostet dass pfoont (keelo, leeter)?
Drinking water, milk, tea, coffee .	**Trinkwasser, Milch, Tee, Kaffee**
	trinkvahsser, milsh, tay, kafay
Wine, beer, cider	**Wein, Bier, Apfelwein**
	vine, beer, apfel-vine
The bill, please	**Bitte bezahlen**
	bitta betsahlen

Money, Shopping

Money, coin, note	**Geld, Münze, Geldschein**
	gelt, mintza, geltshine
I want some—	**Ich brauche—**
	ish browka—
How much is this (are these)? . . .	**Was kostet dies (kosten diese)?**
	vahss kostet dees (kosten deeza)?
Can you change—?	**Können Sie—wechseln?**
	kennen zee—vexeln?
Stationer	**Schreibwarenhändler**
	shripewahren-hendler
writing-paper	**Schreib-papier**
	shripe-papeer
ink, envelopes	**Tinte, Umschläge**
	tinta, oomshlayga
Postcards	**Postkarten**
	postkarten
The hairdresser	**Der Friseur**
	dair freezeer

54

I want a haircut (shampoo)	**Bitte das Haar schneiden (ein Shampoo)** *bitt*a dass hahr *shny*den (ine sham*poo*)
I want a shave	**Bitte mich rasieren** *bitt*a mish raz*ee*ren
Tobacconist, cigarettes, cigar, matches	**Tabakhändler, Zigaretten, Zigarre, Streichhölzer** *tabahk-hend*ler, *tsi*garetten, tsig*ahr*a, *shtrysh*-hultser
Pipe-tobacco	**Pfeifentabak** *pfy*fen-tabahk

Entertainment

Theatre, cinema, music-hall	**Theater, Kino, Variété** tay*ah*ter, *keen*o, vareeay*tay*
What time does the show begin?	**Wann beginnt die Vorstellung?** vahn be*ginnt* dee *fore*shtelloong?
What price are the seats?	**Was kosten die Plätze?** vahss *kos*ten dee *pletz*a?
Broadcasting, programme, wireless set	**Radio, Programm, Radioempfänger** *rah*deeoh, pro*gramm*, *rah*deeoh-emp*feng*er

The Post Office

Where is the post office?	**Wo ist das Postamt?** vo ist dass *post-ahmt*
Number engaged, delay	**Nummer besetzt, Verzögerung** *noom*er be*zetst*, fair*tsee*ge-roong

Public Notices

Notice, advertisement.	**Anschlag, Anzeige**
	*ahn*shlahk, *ahn*tsyga
It is forbidden	**Es ist verboten**
	ess ist fair*boh*ten
Smoking (spitting) forbidden.	**Rauchen (Spucken) verboten**
	*row*ken (*shpook*en) fair*boh*ten
Entrance free, entrance forbidden	**Eintritt frei, Eintritt verboten**
	*ine*tritt fry, *ine*tritt fair*boh*ten
Stopping-place, (bus, tram)	**Haltestelle, Strassenbahn**
	*hahl*ta-*shtell*a, *shtrah*ssenbahn
Bus	**Omnibus**
	omni*booss*
Do not touch, keep off the grass, high tension	**Nicht berühren, den Rasen nicht betreten, Hochspannung**
	nisht be*reer*en, dain *rah*zen nisht be*tray*ten, *hohk*shpannoong
Private property	**Privateigentum**
	pree*vaht*-eyegentoom
Ladies, Gentlemen	**Damen, Herren**
	*dah*men, *hair*en
Vacant, engaged	**Frei, besetzt**
	fry, be*zetst*
Open, closed	**Offen, geschlossen**
	*off*en, ge*shloss*en

Accidents

Where is the doctor (chemist)	**Wo ist der Arzt (Apotheker)?**
	vo ist daair artst (appo*taker*)
Fetch a doctor, please.	**Bitte holen Sie einen Arzt**
	*bitt*a *hoh*len zee *eye*nen artst

56

Help quickly	**Helfen Sie schnell** *helf*en zee shnell
There has been an accident . .	**Ein Unfall ist geschehen** ine *oon*fall ist ge*shay*en
I have been wounded (injured) .	**Ich bin verwundet (verletzt)** ish bin fair*voon*det (fair*letst*)
Fever	**Fieber** *fee*ber
It hurts me here	**Ich have [*sic*] Schmerzen hier** ish *hah*ba *shmairt*sen here
I have broken my arm (cut myself)	**Ich habe den Arm gebrochen (mich geschnitten)** ish *hah*ba dain arm ge*brohk*en (mish ge*shnitt*en)
I have sprained my ankle . . .	**Ich habe das Fussgelenk verrenkt** ish *hah*ba dass *foos*gelenk fair*renkt*
Hand, finger, leg, wrist	**Hand, Finger, Bein, Handgelenk** hahnt, *fing*er, bine, *hahnt*-gelenk
Ankle, foot, thigh, knee	**Fussgelenk, Fuss, Oberschenkel, Knie** *fooss*-gelenk, fooss, *ohber*shenkel, knee
Back, bone, elbow, shoulder . .	**Rücken, Knochen, Ellbogen, Schulter** *rick*en, *knock*en, *ell*bohgen, *shool*ter
Head, neck, face, nose	**Kopf, Hals, Gesicht, Nase** kopf, halss, ge*zisht*, *nahe* [*sic*]
Artery, tourniquet	**Schlagader, Aderpresse** *shlahg*-ahder, *ahder*-pressa
Bandage, ointment, medicine .	**Binde, Salbe, Medizin** *binn*da, *zal*ba, meddit*seen*

Numbers

Number = **Zahl**
tsahl

1 =	**eins**	eyenss
2 =	**zwei**	tsvy
3 =	**drei**	dry
4 =	**vier**	feer
5 =	**fünf**	finf
6 =	**sechs**	zex
7 =	**sieben**	*zee*ben
8 =	**acht**	ahkt
9 =	**neun**	noyn
10 =	**zehn**	tsain
11 =	**elf**	elf
12 =	**zwölf**	tsvelf
13 =	**dreizehn**	*dry*tsain
14 =	**vierzehn**	*feer*tsain

15 =	**fünfzehn**	*finf*tsain
17 =	**siebzehn**	*zeeb*tsain
16 =	**sechsehn**	*zesh*tsain
18 =	**achtzehn**	*ahk*tsain
19 =	**neunzehn**	*noyn*tsain
20 =	**zwanzig**	*tsvahn*tsish
21 =	**ein-und-zwanzig**	ine-oont-*tsvahn*tsish
22 =	**zwei-und-zwanzig**	tsvy-oont-*tsvahn*tsish
23 =	**drei-und-zwanzig**	dry-oont-*tsvahn*tsish
30 =	**dreissig**	*dry*sish
40 =	**vierzig**	*feer*tsish
50 =	**fünfzig**	*finf*tsish
60 =	**sechzig**	*zesh*tsish
70 =	**siebzig**	*zeeb*tsish
80 =	**achtzig**	*ahk*tsish

90 =	**neunzig**	125 =	**hundert-fünf-und-zwanzig**
	*noyn*tsish		*hoond*ert-finf-oont-*tsvahn*tsish
100 =	**hundert**	200 =	**zwei hundert**
	*hoond*ert		tsvy *hoond*ert
101 =	**hundert-eins**	1,000 =	**tausend**
	*hoond*ert-eyenss		*tow*zend

Once =	**einmal**	Ten times =	**zehnmal**
	*ine*mahl		*tsain*mahl
Twice =	**zweimal**	A half =	**ein Halb**
	*tsvy*mahl		ine halp
Three times =	**dreimal**	A third =	**ein Drittel**
	*dry*mahl		ine *dritt*el
Four times =	**viermal**	A quarter =	**ein Viertel**
	*feer*mahl		ine *feer*tel

Time

One o'clock	**Ein Uhr**
	ine oor
Half past one	**Halb zwei**
	halp tsvy
A quarter past seven	**Viertel acht**
	*feer*tel ahkt
A quarter to nine	**Drei-viertel neun**
	dry-*feer*tel noyn
Ten minutes to ten	**Zehn Minuten vor zehn**
	tsain min*oot*en fore tsain
Five minutes past two	**Fünf Minuten nach zwei**
	finf min*oot*en nahk tsvy
Day, night	**Tag, Nacht**
	tahk, nahkt

59

Moon [*sic*], midnight	**Mittag, Mitternacht**
	*mitt*ahk, *mitt*ernahkt
Today, tomorrow, yesterday . .	**Heute, morgen, gestern**
	*hoy*ta, *morg*en, *gest*ern
Morning, afternoon, evening .	**Morgen, Nachmittag, Abend**
	*morg*en, *nahk*mittahk, *ah*bent
This morning, this evening . .	**Heute morgen, heute Abend**
	*hoy*ta *morg*en, *hoy*ta *ah*bent
To-night	**Heute Nacht**
	*hoy*ta nahkt
What time is it?	**Wie spät ist es?**
	vee shpate ist ess?
Monday, Tuesday, Wednesday .	**Montag, Dienstag, Mittwoch**
	*mohn*tahk, *deens*tahk, *mitt*vock
Thursday, Friday, Saturday . .	**Donnerstag, Freitag, Sonnabend**
	*donn*erstahk, *fry*tahk, *zonn*ahbent
Sunday	**Sonntag**
	*zonn*tahk
This week, last week, next week	**Diese Woche, letzte Woche, nächste Woche**
	*deez*a *vock*a, *lets*ta *vock*a, *naik*sta *vock*a
New Year's Day, Christmas . .	**Neujahrstag, Weihnachten**
	*noy*yahrstahk, *vy*nahkten
Easter, Whitsuntide	**Ostern, Pfingsten**
	*ohs*stern, *pfing*sten

Months and Seasons

January, February, March	**Januar, Februar, März**
	*yan*ooar, *feb*rooar, mairts

60

April, May, June	**April, Mai, Juni**
	app*ril*, my, *yoo*nie
July, August, September. . . .	**Juli, August, September**
	*yoo*lie, *ow*goost, Sep*tem*ber
October, November, December . .	**Oktober, November, Dezember**
	oc*to*ber, no*vem*ber, day*tsem*ber
Winter, Spring.	**Winter, Frühling**
	*vinn*ter, *free*ling
Summer, Autumn	**Sommer, Herbst**
	*zomm*er, hairbst
19th of June, 20th of December. .	**Der neunzehnte June [*sic*], der zwanzigste Dezember**
	dair *noyn*tsainta *yoo*nie, dair *tsvahnt*sicksta day*tsem*ber
11th of January, 14th of November	**Der elfte Januar, der vierzehnte November**
	dair *elf*ta *ya*nooar, dair *feer*tsainta no*vem*ber

Weights and Measures

THESE are based on the decimal Metric System used in most European countries. This is simpler than our British system, since units are all multiples of 10. The equivalents given below are *approximate only*—for quick reckoning.

Length

1 Centimetre (cm.)	1 Zentimeter = two-fifths inch
1 Metre (m. = 100 cms.)	1 Meter = 3 ft. 3 ins.
1 Kilometre (km. = 1,000 ms.)	1 Kilometer = five-eighths mile

To convert *centimetres into inches*—multiply by 4 and divide the result by 10. (1 inch = 2½ cms. 1 foot = 30 cms.)

To convert *metres into yards*—add one-ninth the number of metres.
   (1 yard = nine-tenths of a metre.)
To convert *kilometres into miles*—divide the kms. by 8 and multiply the
   result by 5. (1 mile = just over 1½ kms.)

Weight

1 Gram (g.)	1 Gramm = 15½ grains
1 Kilogram (kg. = 1,000 gs.)	1 Kilogramm (or Kilo.) = 2 lb. 3 oz.
1 Ton	1 Tonne = 1,016 kilos

To convert *kilograms into pounds*—double and then add one-tenth of
   the result. (1 lb. = roughly half a kilo. 1 cwt. = 50 kilos.)
In some parts of Germany the pound (*das Pfund*) = 1 lb. 1½ ozs. is
   commonly used.

Area

1 Hectare   1 Hektare = nearly 2½ acres
To convert *hectares into acres*—multiply by 5, divide by 2.
   (1 acre = two-fifths hectare.)

Liquid Capacity

1 Litre   1 Liter = 1½ pints
To convert *litres into pints*—add half, and then a half of the half.
   (1 pint = just over half a litre.)
To convert *litres into gallons*—divide by 5. (1 gallon = 4½ litres.)

Heat

The measurement used is called Centigrade, by which water freezes at
   0 degrees (instead of our 32° Fahrenheit) and boils at 100° (instead
   of 212° Fahrenheit). Normal body temperature is 37°C.
To convert *Centigrade into Fahrenheit*—double, subtract one-tenth of
   the result and add 32. (100°F. = about 38°C.)

SECURITY NOTE

If there is no open fighting in the part of Germany in which you find yourself you may think that there is no longer any special need for security.

This is not the case. Germans must still be regarded as dangerous enemies until the final Peace Settlement has been concluded and after the occupation of Germany has ended.

Security is therefore as important as ever. In battle, breaches of security may cost men's lives; under conditions behind the line the danger is not so immediate. Such breaches will, however, assist those Germans who are working under-ground against us, and, make no mistake about it, there will be plenty of them.

You will have read in this book all about the character of the Germans, and will know what to expect from them, especially from the Nazi elements. Your attention should therefore be firmly and continually fixed on the following points with regard to which the necessity for security remains paramount:—

1. Attempts by propaganda and agents to secure sympathy for the German people and to convince you that they have had a raw deal.
2. Attempts by propaganda and agents to create ill-feeling between us and our Allies, and in particular to stir up anti-Russian feeling.
3. Attempts to sabotage, and to injure the Allied Forces in Germany.
4. Attempts to obtain information as to the movements, dispositions and activities of our Forces, and other information of a military nature, such as advance information of projected operations, search parties, raids and similar intentions.

63

In order to combat this, you should constantly bear in mind the following:—

Be careful what you say—not only to civilians, but in their hearing. Many more Germans than you think understand and speak English.

Be guarded in what you say on the telephone. Remember that a telephone line is never private.

Remember that propaganda will be used in many forms—some crude and obvious, but much of it subtle and difficult to recognise.

Don't be too ready to listen to stories told by attractive women. They may be acting under orders.

Pay especial attention to security of documents, and don't leave letters and private diaries lying about. Although apparently harmless, they may contain information of value to the enemy.

Report any suspicious characters *at once* to your Unit Security Officer or to a Field Security Officer.

If you have to check identity documents, be scrupulously thorough in assuring yourself that the bearer is all that he claims to be. And finally never leave weapons or ammunition unguarded. Remember the saboteur and the assassin.

Life in Germany will demand your constant vigilance, alertness and self-confidence. Each one of you has a job to do. See that you carry it through, however irksome it may seem, with goodwill and determination. The more thorough we are now the less likely are we to have trouble in the future.